INDIA RISING

INDIA RISING

EMERGENCE OF A NEW WORLD POWER

Tarun Das,
Colette Mathur and Frank-Jürgen Richter

Marshall Cavendish
Business

Cover photo: Lonely Planet Images

Published by Marshall Cavendish Editions
An imprint of Marshall Cavendish International
1 New Industrial Road, Singapore 536196

Other Marshall Cavendish Offices
Marshall Cavendish Ltd. 119 Wardour Street, London W1F OUW, UK • Marshall Cavendish Corporation. 99 White Plains Road, Tarrytown NY 10591-9001, USA • Marshall Cavendish International (Thailand) Co Ltd. 253 Asoke, 12th Flr, Sukhumvit 21 Road, Klongtoey Nua, Wattana, Bangkok 10110, Thailand • Marshall Cavendish (Malaysia) Sdn Bhd, Times Subang, Lot 46, Subang Hi-Tech Industrial Park, Batu Tiga, 40000 Shah Alam, Selangor Darul Ehsan, Malaysia

National Library Board Singapore Cataloguing in Publication Data

Mathur, Colette. India rising / Colette Mathur, Frank-Jürgen Richter and Tarun Das.
- Singapore: Marshall Cavendish Business, 2005.
p. cm.
Includes index.
ISBN: 981-261-196-7

1. India - Economic policy - 1991- 2. India - Economic conditions - 1947- I. Richter, Frank- Jürgen. II. Das, Tarun. III. Title.

HC435.3
338.954 -- dc21 SLS2005045001

Printed in Singapore

India has, since the last few years, been regarded as a vibrant nation, a priority economic partner, a model of democracy, one of the richest sources of knowledge, scientific excellence and innovations, and a cultural leader.

We, the editors, have always believed in India—in its uniqueness, its great people, its wisdom and its dynamic entrepreneurs. We are delighted to see our dream of a strong, emerging India come true and wish the country the very best for all its people.

They deserve it and will make it happen.

Tarun Das, Colette Mathur and Frank-Jürgen Richter

CONTENTS

Foreword

Professor Klaus Schwab
Chairman of the World Economic Forum

Passive, fatalistic and folkloric. Clichés like these, often used to describe India in the media, certainly do not represent the India of today, as can easily be observed when traveling the land from north to south.

If I were to describe this country, which is opening up to the world and sharing its intelligence and power of creativity, I would do it as follows. The India of today is like a beehive overflowing with activity and dynamism. The streets are full of men and women determined and proud to contribute to their country's economic progress and to be closely associated with it. Self-confidence and trust in a better future for all are the driving forces.

The country never sleeps. Even in the middle of the night, there is always bustling activity in the streets of any one of the mega cities. Throughout India, entrepreneurs transform their factories and companies by integrating advanced technology, which they have either imported, or invented in their laboratories. These socially responsible chief executives are always on the lookout for opportunities to create and innovate. They are in search of quality—the best endorsement for the partners from all over the world with whom they work.

Engineers and scientists, trained in universities and institutes that rank among the most prestigious in India and indeed in the world, devote themselves passionately to research. They offer services in ITC, biotechnology, medicine and other sciences, thereby advancing knowledge and scientific progress.

India's civil society comprises numerous organizations whose members work with dedication and generosity, often in partnership with political and business leaders. These social entrepreneurs, idealists but also pragmatists, help the poorest gain access to education and healthcare. The poor are offered opportunities for self-development as well as the chance to improve their living conditions and those of their families and communities.

India's states, led by both male and female chief ministers determined to transform their states into models of economic and social development, are the locomotives of progress. The chief ministers of the states work towards changing the mentality of those most averse to change. In addition, many political decision makers have revised their list of concerns, placing the country's economic and social development at the top of their priorities.

Finally, we owe India respect for having preserved its many worthy values. These are values of knowledge, family values and ancestral traditions, spiritual and religious tolerance, appreciation of culture and the arts, the importance of education and workmanship and above all, respect for the individual and for life in all its diverse forms.

India deserves greater recognition. We should express our admiration and gratitude to India for all that this great country has contributed to the world—the arts, the sciences and philosophy.

I am grateful to everyone involved in publishing or contributing to this book. It is very well timed as the world finally realizes that India is indeed becoming a new world power.

Preface

Dr. Manmohan Singh
Prime Minister of India

I am pleased to learn that the Confederation of Indian Industry (CII) and the World Economic Forum are commemorating two decades of their association and their joint sponsorship of the India Economic Summit by publishing a book on India's emergence as an important economic player in the world economy.

I have had the good fortune of participating in many of the events organized by the CII and the World Economic Forum over the past two decades. These events have been milestones for our businesses on their journey of enterprise and creativity. I recall the initial conferences when Rajiv Gandhi was our prime minister and the new vision he gave us for our journey into the 21st century. CII has been an important forum for debate on Rajiv's ideas in the areas of economic reform and liberalization. On that foundation of modernism and liberal economic policies, we have started, since 1991, to build a strong edifice with the government implementing major initiatives. I recall with gratitude the support offered to us by CII and the World Economic Forum as they spread our message of change to businesses across the country and around the world.

India has changed remarkably. The far-reaching changes after 1991 have made our economy more competitive and encouraged Indian enterprises to compete with the best in the world. New benchmarks for performance were set and as we look back today, we should justifiably feel proud of all that we have achieved.

The Indian economy is stronger today than ever before. Both our manufacturing and services sectors have managed to address the challenges of modernization and global competition. The share of foreign trade in our national income has doubled. Our share of world trade in goods and services has increased. Partnering the government, the CII and the World Economic Forum have been immensely important in this process of change. For this, we are very appreciative.

There are, however, unaddressed issues and new challenges facing India. There has been a relative neglect of the agrarian economy and of employment generation. There has also been a neglect of social infrastructure and human development.

We now endeavor to address these challenges. We are committed to a more humane and equitable process of economic development that would enable the economy to grow at 7% to 8% per year; and, make India more open to international flows of capital and goods and more cognizant of the domestic challenges of social and economic justice.

The Indian economy is fast emerging as a major player in the global economy and in global economic institutions. We believe that a rule-based multilateral trading regime is in our interests. We are also committed to closer economic interactions with our Asian neighbors as well as new and traditional economic partners.

India's global profile has recently been enhanced by the impressive reputation of our professionals in the knowledge economy, in fields such as information technology, biotechnology, finance and commerce.

Both the CII and the World Economic Forum have my good wishes in all their future endeavors to promote India and the opportunities we offer to businesses at home and abroad.

Part 1

Introduction

INDIA CAUGHT THE WORLD BY SURPRISE

by Colette Mathur and Frank-Jürgen Richter

The surprising pickup in India's economy over the last few years may herald a new era of growth provided that the political and economic landscape, now more business-friendly, also succeed in lifting the nation's social conditions.

We have grown accustomed to India's low growth rates, its notorious barriers to entrepreneurship and its resistance to foreign business. Internal political concerns and interests had always appeared to take far too much precedence over economic priorities.

We have, however, witnessed a recent acceleration in India's economic momentum. The upheaval stems from a liberalization process that began nearly 15 years ago. It is a process which has gained pace over time, fueled by the need for economic reforms and India's desire to play a larger role on the global political and economic stage.

Headline economic figures and analyses show impressive economic performances and changes conducive to the business environment. A closer look, however, at the lives of the hundreds of millions of Indian poor clustered in city slums and rural expanses will show little if no real change. Despite a burgeoning middle-class, India's recent growth story has yet to be known by the poorest population mass. The surprising results of the latest general elections in 2004 was in part an expression and response to this.

The elections are also a reminder of how true a democracy India is. By reversing the balance of power, the Indian people sent a strong message to the nation's leaders. Economic success and growth—'India shining'—need to reach out further into the country.

FROM WHERE HAS INDIA COME?

Throughout most of the second half of the 20th century, the low rates of Indian growth led economic and political observers to assume that India was simply unable to tap into its economic potential. It was commonly accepted that the 'infamous' criterion, the Hindu growth rate of 3-4% a year, was an inevitable given.

The contrast with Southeast Asian developing nations has been striking. Countries such as South Korea and Singapore, as poor and underdeveloped as India in the 1950s, grew to become successful economies and joined the OECD.

Economic and political observers have often speculated whether a developing country of the size and diversity of India could achieve high growth rates if it was not under an authoritarian regime. There are many examples, within Asia, of this latter route to economic development. The next 20 to 30 years will determine how sustainable these models are and how they survive the inevitable transition towards democracy.

India's economic and political landscape cannot be compared to that of other developing nations'. It has been modeled on economic, financial and political choices, but shaped by competing ideological, cultural and religious influences. Its foundations and ways of functioning are so unique that it would be easiest to describe these as products of 'indianity'.

But with GDP growth rates ranging between 7 and 8% in 2003 and 2004, India seems to have finally found its way to development. This could become a unique model in economic history—a model based fully on democratic values and driven by the people and the diverse communities ('bottom up'), rather than imposed by a strong central authority.

To get a better understanding of the underlying structures governing India's economy today, one needs some insight into its historical background and influences.

A KNOWLEDGE AND CASTE-BASED SOCIETY

The beginnings of the Indian civilization can be traced back to 2500 BC, with the organization of commerce and agriculture within the Indus Valley. Mankind's earliest written books, the *Vedas*, were found.on this land.

Aryans invaded the land around 1500 BC, bringing with them a new culture and a new language—Sanskrit. In the following centuries, successive wars, invasions and encounters with other cultures, such as the Dravidian culture, led to the emergence of a society ruled by castes. These castes were based on occupational specializations and were dominated by the upper classes. Successive cultures attempted to put an end to the system without success. Among these, adepts of Buddhism (which was founded in India by Siddhartha Gautama in the 5th century BCE) fought the caste system. But the Hindu caste system persisted, and even outlived Muslim influence which started with Arab and Turkish incursions in the 8th century, and lasted right up to the end of the Mogul empire in the 19th century.

Despite the negative connotations associated with the Indian caste system today, it is this very system that served as the fabric and support for Indian civilization across centuries. The caste system evolved on the basis of specialized expertise and talents, which were passed from father to son. To some extent, the system is comparable to the 'corporatization' that took place in the Middle Ages in Europe which was also based on occupational specializations.

Indian society has, of course, evolved over the last centuries. While the caste system remains an important social and economic anchor, its grip on people's destiny has diminished. Driven and enterprising individuals have a better chance today than ever before of breaking away from lives initially imposed by caste and family, and forging their own career paths. Regional and national mobility has increased, as individuals leave predetermined ties behind and seek opportunities elsewhere. This is not to say, obviously, that the socially and financially elevated have lost their privileged access to education and job opportunities.

Knowledge and the sciences have remained highly admired throughout India's history. Weak economic progress in India until the end of the 20th century cannot be attributed to a shortfall of talent or to the effects of India's social structures and diversified culture.

THE IMPRINT OF COLONIZATION

At the dawn of the modern world, British colonization, which began in the 17th century, froze Indian social structures in place for over 200 years. A repressed society weighed down by British domination and control, India was unable to evolve and progress.

Emerging from British rule, there was little industry and commerce to speak of when India gained its independence in 1947. The nation's intellectual and scientific potential remained unexplored. The middle-class was a tiny minority and over 90% of the population was spread over poor and totally underdeveloped villages. Additionally, economic activities were hampered by a strict bureaucracy imposed by the British rulers, which was maintained in India and is still partly in place today.

The effects of colonization were to have a major and determining impact on India's economic and political policies following its independence. British oppression and economic exploitation led to the emergence of the Indian 'swadeshi' socio-economic philosophy. This philosophy in effect translates into local self-sufficiency and was central to Mahatma Gandhi's call for the unity of the Indian people and the assertion of Indian pride throughout the struggle for independence. Gandhi's movement encouraged the practice of promoting and consuming Indian-made goods, by replacing, for instance, British textiles with homespun cloths.

INDEPENDENT AND DEMOCRATIC INDIA

In 1949, two years after independence, India's Constitution was enacted by the 'constituent assembly' and it took effect on 26 January, 1950.

The Constitution defines India as a sovereign, socialist and secular government. India is a federal democratic republic comprising 28 states, six union territories and NCT Delhi. The Indian parliament is composed of two chambers. The Rajya Sabha (or council of states) consists of 250 members elected or designated by the president, while the Lok Sabha (house of representatives) consists of 543 members elected from the states and union territories. A regionally elected chief minister leads each state.

Ever since independence, India has both impressed and intrigued the world by being the largest effective democracy in the world. Throughout its modern history, it has demonstrated its commitment to democratic values that reach across its multiple ethnic and religious communities. The current political environment is a good illustration of this diversity as the nation has a Muslim president and a Sikh prime minister, and at the helm of a leading political party, a president of Italian origin.

The economic consequences, however, stemming from a democratic government needing to manage centralized and socialist policies across a nation as large as India (a task made unwieldy by India's diversity), are obvious and inevitable in hindsight. This political environment invited the growth of bureaucracy, corruption and inefficiency.

INDEPENDENT AND SOCIALIST INDIA

With its destiny in its own hands and under its control, India now had to find its path to nation-building. The Indian National Congress Party, which was the leading body in India's independence movement, formed the first government. India's first prime minister, Jawaharlal Nehru, steered the nation towards the then highly influential Russian socialist, central planning economic model. Remembering the oppression of colonization, the nation maneuvered itself well clear of western influence and the capitalism associated with it. The 'swadeshi' philosophy reduced India's imports, providing a protected market for domestic producers.

The 'planning commission', which was created during Nehru's leadership, orchestrated and centralized government policy. It elaborated five-year plans, setting economic priorities and targets. The 'planning commission' remains central to government policy making today, albeit to a lesser extent.

The new government channeled public resources towards growing a nationalized heavy industry sector. India thus embarked on the road to becoming a new industrial power. India's first government also set its priorities on reforming the agricultural sector. Land was redistributed to the labor force, and public funds were allocated to introduce modern irrigation, fertilization and other enhanced techniques. In a certain sense, India was undergoing its own 'green revolution'. Famines that had plagued the land for centuries were greatly reduced and, a point of national pride, India achieved self-sufficiency in food.

Education was also a top priority on Nehru's economic and political agenda. It was during the 1950s and 1960s that the first universities and research institutes were founded. Today, these constitute the pillars of India's highly respected academia.

Nehru's socialist policies were pursued and extended by his successors right up to and during the premiership of Mrs. Indira Gandhi, but they increasingly stifled entrepreneurship and private enterprise. Mounting economic regulations and bureaucracy (with the corruption that comes with it) progressively crowded out the market economy. Price controls, quotas, license requirements, bureaucratic weight and associated corruption placed a notorious number of obstacles in the way of private enterprise. This bureaucratic 'license raj' system, over-regulation and protectionism hindered India's innovative and competitive potential. Large, politically-privileged enterprises benefited from the system, at a cost to smaller businesses and consumers. The former established inefficient monopolies in the domestic industrial and commercial sectors, produced goods of poor quality, and had protectionism as their guard against international competition.

THE GEOPOLITICAL SITUATION

Geopolitical factors have always been a hindrance to India's economic progress. Among the most important of these has been India's unstable geopolitical situation.

Since its independence, India has found itself in conflict with neighboring nations. At war once with China and thrice with Pakistan, India's regional conflicts persist to date. These tensions have burdened national resources and are a distraction from economic priorities. This burden has been particularly important right through to the end of Indira Gandhi's rule.

In summary, rigid social structures, nationalism, ineffective centralized socialist policies, and a host of religious, regional and geopolitical tensions have hampered India's economic and social progress. They have burdened India with inadequate infrastructure, labor market rigidities, regulatory problems and foreign trade and investment controls.

These various elements certainly contributed to India's low annual economic growth rates that averaged 3.5% between the early 1950s and early 1980s.

THE ECONOMY—MODELING INDIA'S ECONOMIC DEVELOPMENT

Following Indira Gandhi's assassination in 1985, her son, 40-year-old Rajiv Gandhi, became prime minister. He enjoyed a clean reputation and his eagerness to drive the country forward created a new climate of confidence and optimism. His popularity empowered the Congress party and its large majority in parliament in subsequent elections, and sanctioned a mandate for change.

His first task was to reform his party, the Indian National Congress Party, and transform it into an efficient political force supporting his national, regional and international initiatives.

Together with his administration, he led India on its first steps towards economic liberalization. To encourage private enterprise and reduce tax evasion, both corporate and income taxes were cut to 40%. Rajiv's liberalization measures also covered industrial policy, easing licensing laws for small enterprises and reducing the scope and power of the monopolies' watchdog. India started to move slowly towards the international economic scene by reducing certain import tariffs and quotas, and allowing tie-ups with foreign companies.

Rajiv's personal interest in high technology certainly played a key role in drawing the attention of Indian entrepreneurs and engineers to electronics and software development. Steps to kick-start the IT industry included reducing duties on capital imports, subsidizing research and development on electronics and computer software, as well as revamping India's antiquated public telephone system.

Additionally, under his leadership, the South Asian Association for Regional Cooperation (SAARC) was inaugurated in 1985. Rajiv further developed diplomatic relations with the United States, Europe and Russia, thereby increasing India's international exposure.

Rajiv Gandhi was assassinated in 1991. Economic historians would describe the reforms introduced by his administration as mild and modest. These reforms were effective, however, in driving the first credible acceleration in the nation's economic growth rates. Real GDP growth averaged 5.6% per year during Rajiv Gandhi's administration, while real rupee exports grew to 15% per year.

When Narasimha Rao took office as prime minister in 1991, a public debt crisis threatened India's commitment to the neo-liberal reforms promoted by the World Bank and the IMF. Rao's then finance minister, Dr. Manmohan Singh, established a far-reaching blueprint for India's economic reforms which was targeted at opening and integrating the Indian economy into international economic systems. He presented an 'austerity budget'. Among the measures proposed were reducing government expenditure, deregulating financial and labor markets, liberalizing foreign investment, devaluating the rupee, privatizing public enterprises, modernizing monetary and fiscal policies, reducing controls and trade barriers, and lowering bureaucratic controls.

Consequently, private sector economic activity and foreign investment increased, and economic growth reached an average of 7%. After the Rao government fell, the country went through yet another period of instability, with no real economic plans under the successive governments in power between 1996 and 1998. Economic reforms, once again, were not a priority.

The 1998 national elections carried the nationalistic Bharatiya Janata Party (BJP) to power and Atal Bihari Vajpayee took office as prime minister of India. During its initial years, Vajpayee's government was politically reluctant to pursue economic liberalization. Indeed, the BJP's rise to power may be attributed in part to a revival in India in the 1990s of the 'swadeshi' philosophy.

However, the economic benefits of extending the liberalization reform process drew Vajpayee and his government to shift priorities. Within the first 12 months in office, Vajpayee's government began setting aside protectionist policies and cultural conservatism to focus on economic issues. These 'second generation reforms' included major industrial and external policy deregulation, privatization and tariff-reducing measures.

Reforms to industrial and external policies, including allowing foreign acquisition of Indian companies and abolishing export obligations for foreign companies, triggered a significant increase in foreign direct investment. Privatization and opening up competition in industries such as the telecommunications and financial sectors increased business efficiency and revenue, thereby decreasing the government's fiscal deficit. Investments were also made in overall infrastructure, such as in the construction of new highways, but these have been considered insufficient.

Most importantly, Vajpayee's government is credited with making India a global power in IT, business process outsourcing and biotechnology. Under Vajpayee, India invested massively in technology in four key states. The contribution of Indian IT-related companies to employment and GDP is 3.15%.

The economic reforms carried out by Vajpayee's government were business- and capitalist-friendly, encouraging the spirit and rewards of entrepreneurship. Indian companies started to modernize, integrate new technologies and bring in efficient management. New Indian multinational companies were born. Present in all the markets, they compete very successfully with their foreign peers, and have given India a great competitive advantage over other emerging countries. The reforms also allowed service industries to boom by deregulating the telecommunications sector and facilitating connectivity for the new IT and IT-related companies.

THE STRUCTURE OF THE BOOK

This book is divided into three sections. Part 1 provides an overview of India's economy and discusses the current reform agenda. We look at India's economic history, its general and expected growth path, as well as the potential and underlying model that would achieve this growth. In Part 2, the core of the book, we propose 10 pillars of sustainable growth. Each chapter starts with a scenario[1], followed by two essays discussing the respective

1 The scenarios are the result of a long-term cooperation between the World Economic Forum and the Confederation of Indian Industry (CII). The original versions of the scenarios were developed for the India Economic Summit in 2002 and 2003. The Summit looked at how the Indian economy could fully harness its potential and build on its many competitive advantages. Summit participants used these scenarios as a basis for their interactive debates on the key drivers of growth in India. Since 1986, the World Economic Forum and CII have held the yearly India Economic Summit in New Delhi. With 500 senior business leaders from India and abroad, experts, foreign public personalities, members of the government and senior officials, the gathering is now acknowledged as the most important international business event in India. It benefits from the support of the Indian government and provides the business community with a unique platform to formulate and communicate its concerns and recommendations.

proposals on how to achieve a best-case scenario. The 10 scenarios focus on economic reforms, financial reforms, geopolitics, manufacturing, trade and foreign investment, energy, information technology, agriculture, infrastructure and social issues. The scenarios are stories that describe a possible future in the long-term environment of India's economy. They identify significant events in the country's future, discuss the main actors and their motivations, and convey how India as a whole may function. Senior leaders from the government, business sector, media, academia and civil society, the essayists try to capture the progress made by India to become one of the world's engines for growth. The writers categorize the potential roadblocks of economic growth under the rubric of issues related to sustainability in the development process.

In Part 3, Tarun Das offers a summary and proposes the ways forward. He suggests general policies for India's development that reflect on the scenarios and essays presented in this book. The result is neither a unanimous view of India's future, nor is it a prediction. Rather, it describes a context in which India's economy and society may evolve.

Will India be the new world power? The answer from our contributors and us, the editors, is a resounding yes. India's economy is spawning a growing middle-class, a booming stock market, a host of international companies, and a new image for this nation of more than one billion people. Nonetheless, Indians have to continue trying hard to improve the conditions for further sustainable growth as the country is susceptible to religious riots, secessionist movements, urban squalor and bitter rural poverty, as is evident from its history.

What is needed is better coordination between central and local authorities, more efficient means of attracting FDI (foreign direct investment), and a generally better-functioning bureaucracy. The New Indian development model shall finally abandon the dogmatic focus on 'swadeshi'.

CAN WE SPEAK OF AN INDIAN MIRACLE?

Economic and political headlines speak of an 'Indian miracle', based on an 8% GDP growth rate, a well-controlled 5% inflation rate and the rise of foreign reserves to well above US$100 billion. The growing middle-class has become a huge domestic market of 300 million, while the services sector, which accounts for 50% of GDP, has been driving exports higher. Some of India's largest corporations have grown able to compete with the world's largest multinationals.

However, the rewards of this progress have yet to benefit the masses. Access to adequate electricity, water, higher education and healthcare remains a privilege. Public services and basic infrastructure are largely inadequate, while private sector products hardly reach the poorest. Over 20% of India's population live below the World Bank-defined 'poverty line'. Overall social conditions make India an emerging/'third world' nation.

The sustainability of accelerating growth rates will clearly require continued progress in the liberalization process. Current and future governments, however, face the mounting challenge posed by the cost of an economic divide. India's leap in information technology and globalization has carried news of India's successes and new wealth to the homes of those left behind. The latter carry enough weight in India's democracy to punish businesses and economy-friendly governments if the effects of welfare policies do not benefit them. Clearly, overall welfare must yet improve to provide further support for market-oriented reforms.

This will obviously call for policies that allow a higher and faster diffusion rate of wealth to the poor. It will also require a dramatic improvement in public goods services—roads, electricity, water—as shortfalls in basic infrastructure also continue to hinder the lives of the middle-class.

The newly elected government led by Prime Minister Manmohan Singh, and many other governments to come, will have to reinvent the India model. Maintaining the momentum of economic reforms, preserving India's leadership in services and ICT, and in other high technology industries, attracting foreign investment and maintaining high levels of economic growth remain absolute necessities for Indian industrialists, and small and medium enterprises, to be competitive. These efforts in turn will support much-needed job creation through, for instance, the development of infrastructure and the greater investment in social sectors such as education and healthcare, and provide for the basic needs of the population at large. Knowing the intelligence, talents, imagination and creativity of the Indian people, we are sure that India will once again surprise us. India has skilfully maintained important values throughout its history, including democracy; respect and admiration for 'learned people'; acceptance of other cultures and religions; tolerance for the 'other'; close family ties; as well as caring for the elderly and less fortunate. These, along with the many other distinctive qualities of Indian society, will enable leaders from all walks of life, whether from the public or private sectors or from civil society, to find ways to ensure that all Indians live in dignity and have a chance to benefit from and contribute to India's further economic and social development.

It is likely that India's growth path will be a very lasting and sustainable one. India will continue to evolve rapidly. The market and the competitive landscape will continue to change. It is now vital that all those involved in India's development, in India and abroad, keep their mind as open as possible about the many opportunities and risks that naturally accompany such historical development. The task to transform India into one of the world's leading economies is formidable, exhausting and filled with obstacles. It is the book's aim to contribute to this task. Welcome to the economic transformation of the millennium!

Part 2

The 10 Pillars for Sustainable Growth

ECONOMIC REFORMS

Scenario

Tarun Das
Chief Mentor, Confederation of Indian Industry

The growth of the economy has always been a sensitive and important issue, especially in a developing country like India. There is a lot of concern among the policymakers as well as the general public regarding the factors that may enhance or hamper the growth of the economy. This paper tries to analyze a few such factors, and tries to draw some estimates on how the performance of various sectors of the economy may affect the overall growth. We consider three scenarios, each with a different GDP growth rate (5.5%, 6.5% and 8%, respectively), and then estimate the growth rates that may be required in the sub-sectors of the economy in order to achieve the GDP growth rates of the three scenarios.

First of all, we take a quick look at the macro conditions that have prevailed in the economy from 1991 to 2002. We observe that inflation rates have been low for most of this period, and this trend is expected to continue in the coming years. The balance of payment situation has been quite comfortable. Monetary and exchange rate policies have been effective. Overall, the financial sector can be described as being very healthy.

The other important broad sector of the economy is the infrastructure sector. In this sector, the telecommunications and highway programs have performed well. Though the performance of the power sector has been highly unsatisfactory, the underlying causes are more political in nature than economic.

Another area that has been a cause of much concern is the fiscal health of the economy. Deficits have been alarmingly high, and given the present trends, this situation is only expected to deteriorate. Finally, the manufacturing sector. This sector has contributed significantly to the growth of the economy. Over the 1991-2002 period, the years of high growth were characterized by high growth in the manufacturing industry, regardless of growth performance in the agriculture industry.

For our analysis, we peg the savings rate at 23.4% of GDP, following recent data. Further, investment rates are taken to be 24.5%, 25.5% and 26.5% of GDP, corresponding with GDP growth rates of 5.5%, 6.5% and 8% respectively. We also project the value of total GDP and GDP per capita for the year 2015, for each of the three scenarios. The figures are given in the table below. Note that the GDP in the year 2003 was $528 billion and the per capita GDP was $497. All the figures are at constant 1995 prices.

Growth Rate (%)	Total GDP ($ billion, at constant 1995 prices)	GDP per capita ($, at constant 1995 prices)
5.5	1,003	791
6.5	1,108	873
8.0	1,262	995

We recognize that several reform processes may need to be undertaken for the economy to achieve the targeted growth rates. The first growth target of 5.5% may not require significant reforms. This target may be achieved given the current situation where growth is the direct result of the sheer size of the market; demand and supply conditions; and some contribution from the unfettered services sector. On the other hand, a growth rate of 6.5% would require some reforms and these should proceed at a greater pace. In addition, there should be enough growth in infrastructure and foreign investments.

Finally, to achieve a growth rate of 8%, a major economic overhaul is required. For this, it is important that India fully masters the political economy and rhetoric of reforms. The pace of reform must be made significantly greater, and all second-stage reforms must be in place. It also requires major breakthroughs in physical, financial and social infrastructure. The parliament should pass most, if not all, key reform legislations. All this would lead to major all-round improvement in governance.

If the country manages to undertake these reforms, then the ensuing changes in the economy would result in high growth rates. These changes would be in terms of the growing size of the domestic and international markets, and increased efficiencies. Most barriers to growth would be reduced, if not eliminated fully. There would not be any significant opposition to goods and factor market reforms. Substantive growths in infrastructure and foreign investments would be observed. Also, regulations over the agricultural sector would be relaxed, and rural incomes raised. Apart from the huge growth in services, growth of at least 10% in manufacturing would also be observed.

All these reforms are definitely expected to have an impact on the growth in GDP. The removal of product market barriers is expected to stimulate GDP growth by at least 1% after three to five years. The privatization of central government-controlled state-owned enterprises alone could bring about at least 0.3% growth in GDP as it encourages greater productivity. In addition, the efficiency gains from the systematic privatization of power distribution are estimated at an extra 0.5% of GDP growth. Investments in building infrastructure such as roads and railways should contribute to an additional GDP growth of at least 1% per year. To this may be added another 0.2% accruing from better ports and airports. Over time, improvements in land reforms should raise GDP growth by an extra 0.5% per year. In the end, we also note that these reforms are not difficult to implement. Together, they can generate an extra 3.5% GDP growth, which would help in achieving the target of 8% growth rate.

Apart from the abovementioned reforms and the resulting changes, it is equally important that the different constituent sectors of the economy contribute towards economic growth. Thus, we proceed to estimate the growth rates that particular sectors need to achieve in order to meet the overall targets specified earlier. Industry is expected to play an important role in the process.

Corresponding to the three scenarios at the macro level, industry has to grow at 5.5%, 8% and 11% respectively. Further, for a high GDP growth rate of 8%, the share of industry in the GDP should gradually increase from 25% in 2002 to 38% in 2015. Moreover, since manufacturing constitutes 70% of Indian industry, a high growth in manufacturing is essential for 11% industry growth. For the agriculture sector, it is assumed that it cannot grow more than 3% per annum. As far as the services sector is concerned, it had been growing at a stable rate of 6% per annum in the past. This must increase to 7%, 7.5% and 9% to achieve the GDP growth rates for the three projected scenarios.

It is evident from the above discussion that industry has a definite role to play in the overall growth. Hence, we may go on to quantify the growth generated in the industrial sector from improvements in certain areas.

First of all, we note that rationalization of energy costs and regulatory issues will raise industrial growth by at least 1.5% per year. Making credit available at international interest rates will stimulate investment and raise industrial growth by at least 1% per year. Maintaining logistic infrastructure will boost industrial performance by at least 1.5% per year. Introduction of a comprehensive VAT across states will reduce compliance costs, remove price distortions and make the whole industry more competitive. This can contribute an additional 1% to industrial growth in the medium to long term. Reforms to reduce regulatory hassles will help the investment climate in the country by accelerating domestic investment and bringing in more FDI; this can contribute an additional 0.5% to industrial growth. In aggregate, this would amount to an additional growth of 5.5% which can increase the total industrial growth rate to more than 11% per annum. However, it is important to recognize that all these issues need to be addressed simultaneously.

We may conclude by observing that to achieve high growth rates in India, it is necessary to implement some strong and non-reversible reforms in certain key areas of the economy. This would determine the growth trajectory that the country follows.

Comment

Suman K. Bery
Director General, National Council of Applied Economic Research (NCAER)

India's economic performance in the 1990s is well-known to most interested observers. A quick and relatively painless adjustment to the balance of payments crisis of 1991 was followed by an investment and output boom. However, after 1997, there was a perceptible slowdown in private investment, and in growth of output in both agriculture and manufacturing. Continued growth in the services sector, both domestic and exported, has been a bright spot, but there are questions whether this performance is sustainable in the absence of strong growth in either manufacturing or agriculture. After consolidation in the early 1990s, the fiscal position deteriorated at both the center and the states. Steady progress was maintained in disinflation and in reducing external vulnerability through a strengthening balance of payments, management of external debt and growth of international reserves.

Against this background, over the last 18 months, there has been a shift of sentiment and a renewal of optimism. An excellent monsoon (both in quantum and in spatial distribution) in the summer of 2003 stimulated agricultural output-still an important driver of the domestic economy. International economic conditions have also been relatively benign, with low international interest rates coupled with a recovery in global trade. International financial conditions have permitted a significant easing in domestic monetary policy (despite the need to sterilize a large increase in reserves). The resulting reduction in interest rates was tonic to the economy, boosting consumer demand and corporate profits, and delivering huge capital gains to the banking sector.

While a cyclical recovery is gathering momentum, there remain questions as to whether it is likely to be sustained, and whether India is approaching the 'take-off' phase of Korea and Taiwan a generation earlier, or that of the ASEAN countries in the 1980s and China in the 1990s. In its 10th Five-Year Plan, India has established an official goal of 8% growth for the country for the period 2002/03 to 2006/07. Others are more bullish: the World Economic Forum (WEF) India Economic Summit in 2002 explored sustaining 8% growth for not just five but 20 years; a recent lecture by the advisor to the Finance Minister[1] suggested that labor force and productivity trends make a 10% growth not impossible; while a study by Goldman Sachs[2] is equally optimistic about the long-run prospects for the Indian economy, for many of the same reasons.

The other papers in this volume discuss the reform agenda in the individual areas in some depth. Professor Kennedy's piece succinctly summarizes the underlying logic of the reform strategy and its link with trade and investment, while Mr. Berkeley's article correctly describes the scepticism expressed by many Indians that the reform challenge will in fact be grasped by the policy establishment. In this essay, I would like to examine the roles that macro policy and economic reform need to play in prolonging the recovery and in fostering rapid medium-term growth. To do so, I focus on three issues:

1) The links between reform and growth
2) Issues of coherence and sequencing
3) Issues of implementation and political management

REFORM AND GROWTH

For growth to be sustained, societies need incentives to encourage the accumulation of factors of production (essentially skilled labor, knowledge and capital). As Professor Kennedy notes, what is even more important is the facilitation of continuous increases in the productivity of these factors. Ultimately, it is only in raising productivity (what economists call total factor productivity) that sustained increases in living standards can be achieved.

Both factor accumulation and increases in productivity raise the supply potential of the economy. For this supply to be reflected in actual

1 Kelkar, Vijay. (2004). "India on a Growth Turnpike". K.R. Narayanan Oration 2004, Australian National University, Canberra.
2 Goldman Sachs, New York. (2003). "Dreaming of BRICs".

output, there must be adequate demand. In the long run (say a 20-year horizon), a focus on the supply side of the economy is entirely valid. But the economy's actual growth performance is also shaped significantly by developments on the demand side. Both sets of policies need to be mutually supportive and internally consistent to generate the desired outcome in terms of actual growth performance. It is, after all, only actual growth performance that can generate the improvements in welfare–the objective of economic growth.

Ensuring consistency in the management of both supply and demand is not easy either in theory or in practice. There are numerous examples available to illustrate this. The IMF was criticized when it stressed structural reform in the aftermath of the Asian crisis in the late 1990s, at a time when the priority should have been in restoring macro-economic equilibrium. Equally, Argentina, which was fairly aggressive on structural reforms, nonetheless suffered a devastating setback because of its macro-economic vulnerabilities. Chile is another ultimately successful Latin American country that initially found it difficult to maintain the balance between structural change and financial stability. South Africa could perhaps be cited as a country with sound and prudent macro policies, but it has nonetheless found growth elusive. China has so far seemed able to power ahead notwithstanding significant distortions on both the structural and macro-economic fronts. Economists continue to disagree sharply on whether Japan's stagnation over the 1990s (now apparently coming to an end) was primarily due to macro-economic factors (deflation, or the so-called Keynesian liquidity trap) or structural rigidity; the answer surely has to be both.

The main point is that there are no certain recipes for sustained growth of the kind that East Asia seemed to have achieved in the 1980s and China more recently. While there may be certain necessary conditions (such as the absence of war, or macro-economic stability), it is difficult to prescribe sufficient conditions. There is instead a need for careful, continuous analyses of individual country situations as these evolve.

A related issue is what weight should be given to stability versus volatility in growth. India has had a traditional preference for stability, but it could well be that a higher average growth performance would require a greater acceptance of volatility. In this regard, India in 2004 is a fundamentally different country (and perhaps less well understood) than the India of 10 years earlier.

In order to get a sense of the interplay between demand and supply factors, and to develop a sense of priority and sequencing, it is useful to review the last business cycle. India's industrial slowdown began in 1997 when world trade and output were growing rapidly. Industrial recovery started in 2001 when the world economy was still weak. It seems reasonable to conclude, therefore, that domestic, rather than international, factors remain of primary significance in determining Indian economic activity, even though international linkages have grown rapidly over the decade.

Within the domestic sphere, several overlapping forces seem to have been at work in generating the slowdown. These include over-investment in the initial boom following liberalization, the tightening of monetary policy after 1996 (out of fear of inflation) and increased political and policy uncertainty. Some of the slowdown can also be attributed to a series of negative shocks that the economy suffered: the impact of economic sanctions following nuclear tests in 1998; the bursting of the IT bubble in the West; the East Asian financial crisis and its impact on demand and competitiveness of India's exports; and a series of indifferent monsoons prior to 2003.

While it is difficult to assign weights to these factors, a focus on the macro economy, particularly the linkage between fiscal outcomes, monetary policy and the exchange rate compels special attention for various reasons. First, the slowdown in industry was fairly widespread across sectors. This suggests that economy-wide factors (rather than just sector-specific factors) were at least partly at work. Second, the last two years have been marked by virtual balance in the current account of the balance of payments. This, coupled with a large build-up of foreign exchange reserves, imply a capital account surplus. While current account surpluses have characterized several other Asian economies in the recent past, it is particularly puzzling in the Indian case, given the continued high levels of fiscal deficit. Given that foreign exchange availability has not been a constraint, the inability of the economy to absorb foreign savings (the mirror image of the current account deficit) is surprising.

It is tempting to conclude that the fiscal deficit (approximately 10% of GDP), largely financed by the issue of bonds placed in the domestic financial market, has been one factor discouraging private investment through high real interest rates. Theory suggests that fiscal deficits will also lead to an appreciation of the real exchange rate, although this is not easy to document on the basis of the indices normally published by the Reserve Bank of India. However, other structural factors are also at play. Trade and investment liberalization, the increased competition they produce and the beginnings of a market in corporate control are all making private business more cautious in its investment decisions. At the same time, domestic banking institutions have been under sustained regulatory pressure to clean up their balance sheets, and have avoided credit expansion out of fear of adding to their bad debts. They have also been encouraged to invest in government debt with the introduction of risk-based capital adequacy norms, which assign zero risk to such investments for purposes of calculating required capital.

I would draw four conclusions from the above analysis. First, a key short-term challenge for India is to re-create a more favorable climate for private sector investment, whether domestic or foreign.

Contrary to the view held in many parts of the Indian private sector, private investment is probably harmed rather than encouraged by excessive fiscal stimuli. Harmful regulatory constraints that remain include continued designation of certain industries for the small-scale sector, rigid labor laws that apply to the organized sector, and a poor legal framework for urban land markets. In addition, poor infrastructure continues to be a major drag on productivity.

Second, the analysis also suggests that in an increasingly market-oriented economy, the short-term link between reform and growth is not a straightforward one. Market-oriented reform often has the effect of increasing the private sector's perceptions of the risks it faces. Indeed, the goal of much reform is often to transfer risks formerly borne by the government to the private sector, on the grounds that the latter will manage the risks better. Unless the private sector is given appropriate instruments and opportunities to handle such risks, reform, while boosting efficiency, may well retard accumulation.

A few examples may help to illustrate this point. Financial sector reforms can be expected to lead to increased volatility in interest rates and exchange rates. Private sector firms need to have access to derivative instruments in order to handle these risks, but provision of such instruments may be discouraged by the regulatory authorities. Increased competition entails an ability to move assets and labor quickly between alternate uses, either within the same firm, or through mergers and acquisitions. If labor market and asset market policies frustrate this re-allocation, the result will be a more cautious attitude toward initial investment, as well as calls for protection under the guise of 'a level playing field'.

Third, reform is dynamic, dangerous and shortlived in its growth impact. By 'dynamic', I mean that the agenda is continually evolving, with one set of reforms begetting the need for further changes. By 'dangerous', I mean that reforms are designed to upset the status quo, and as such, represent a threat to the established order. Hence, they will be resisted. By 'shortlived', I mean that one wave of reforms will provide an initial boost to the economy, but that effect will in time peter out. The true challenge for emerging markets (as for the individual firms within them) is to institutionalize a process of continuous change, and this represents a formidable administrative and political challenge.

The last point is particularly tricky if one considers that, at root, the reforms India needs to undertake entail a redefinition of the role of government (and of the state) in the economy. The state needs to evolve from one concerned with promotion (the absorption of risk) to one concerned with competition (the embrace of risk). This is a difficult transition, both political and conceptual, and it is not surprising that the course is neither smooth nor straightforward. But I would argue that on balance, the experience of the last 10 years—indeed, the last 20 years—gives ample grounds for optimism that the challenges will be met, though not necessarily in a linear or efficient way.

SEQUENCING OF REFORMS

Granting, therefore, that political logic will inevitably be a powerful shaper of what happens, what observations can one offer about the agenda, pace and sequencing of reforms? Thoughts and trends in this area keep evolving in the light of (usually unfortunate) experience. In the early 1990s, partly driven by the circumstances of the 'economies in transition', 'big bang' strategies were in vogue. More than a decade earlier, the relative performance of the Chinese and the Russian economies prompted a more favorable view of a less brusque approach. Indeed, there is nascent literature that cites approvingly the pace and sequencing of India's reforms-a pace that appears painfully slow though to many informed observers, domestic and international.

As per the framework presented above, the objectives of ongoing reform should be to improve the investment climate; enhance productivity of resource use (through increased competition and international specialization); reduce the risks of financial instability; and re-focus state economic activity away from direct action towards competition and poverty alleviation.

As regards the overall incentive regime, the most intricate and interconnected reforms are in the fiscal and financial area, with looser but still important links in the trade and investment regime. There is little doubt that the outcomes on fiscal balance and on public debt have been disappointing at both the central and state levels. This has been so for several reasons. Revenue performance has been weak, partly as there has been no replacement of revenues lost through trade liberalization and through reduction of marginal rates of direct taxes. On the expenditure side, a major autonomous development was in the big increase in public sector wages in 1997. However, financial sector liberalization over the decade has also made explicit the financial repression that was implicit earlier, leading to increases in the interest bill. The relatively poor performance of manufacturing has also contributed to this, as taxation of services is relatively under-developed in India.

For the present, the main negative consequences of the aggregate fiscal position lie in the under-provision of public goods and services rather than the effect on the balance of payments or debt sustainability. But the latter fronts are increasingly vulnerable to a shift in sentiment, or political instability. In addition, indirect taxation can also lead to resource misallocation, regressive incidence, corruption and inefficiency.

While a sharp fiscal adjustment is unlikely, the direction of change needs to be clearly established, both in terms of the pattern of taxation and the aggregate balances. On the revenue side, the challenge is to simultaneously increase the tax to GDP ratio, to reduce the rates and dispersion of customs duties; and to rationalize and clean up the excise duty structure. It is equally important to radically improve tax administration. These challenges have been taken up by several government commissions, the most recent of which were the committees on the reform of direct and indirect taxes (under the chairmanship of Dr. Vijay Kelkar). In the meantime, progress seems to be fitful on the conceptually difficult and politically contentious issue of harmonizing state-level sales taxes with the central excise tax in a VAT (value-added tax)-style crediting structure. It is more difficult to summarize the initiatives in the area of tax administration, but these too will be vital.

Revenue increases need to be supported by privatization and lower interest rates in order to have an impact on public savings and on the overall deficit. In these two areas, there has been progress as well.

A reduced supply of government paper should permit a gradual reduction in real interest rates, creating a virtuous cycle on the fiscal side. For the financial system, this would imply a shift from government paper to more risky loan assets.

But although such a shift is highly desirable from the perspective of the economy as a whole, the existing structure of the banking industry is poorly suited to the emerging financial needs of the economy. While public ownership of the banks has provided a valuable security cushion for depositors over the last decade of financial stress, it has several serious negative implications. Such ownership impedes competition in the banking services industry itself; it complicates the regulatory role of the Reserve Bank of India; it inevitably politicizes the tough commercial decisions that banks should exercise in a market economy as part of an institutional framework that forces resources to earn their appropriate returns; and it prevents the emergence of a structure that is best suited to a dynamic and evolving economy. Unfortunately, while privatization is increasingly accepted in most other areas, in commercial banking, it remains a political impossibility at present. This will be a handicap in the years ahead.

The existing industry structure is also less than ideal for facilitating further integration of the Indian financial system into global markets, a process which is captured by the somewhat loose phrase 'capital account convertibility'. Nonetheless, progress should continue to be made in this area, as it will yield important benefits to India in terms of cost of capital and risk diversification. Given India's strength in other service areas, supply of financial services to the rest of the world seems a likely area of comparative advantage, but this is one that is unlikely to be realized under the present restrictive regime. The so-called capital account convertibility would require greater flexibility in exchange rate policy and appropriate risk management instruments, as discussed earlier.

Trade policy is also intimately linked to this complex of reforms. I have already noted the links between trade policy and the fiscal situation. Trade policy is also a very powerful determinant of the competitiveness of the economy, which in turn is linked to the health of the financial system. Many of the distressed assets carried in the books of the banks and the financial institutions are the result of inappropriate investment decisions undertaken in the more protected era of the early 1990s. These decisions have not proven viable in the more liberal environment of the second half of the decade. India's reform experience differs significantly from emerging markets in both Central Europe and Latin America in that it stretches out the reduction in import duties over a much longer period, to the detriment of both private investment and the health of the financial system.

While all of the above reforms will ultimately support faster growth, it is also the case that they would in turn be facilitated by growth itself. Growth would boost revenues, and reduce the fiscal deficit and debt to GDP ratio. In my view, the easiest and least costly way of administering a positive confidence shock that could jumpstart the growth and investment cycle would be through a major commitment to privatization. I would also be inclined to move faster on external trade and financial liberalization, and on greater exchange rate flexibility.

I have concentrated on this set of reforms for two reasons. First, they are both primordial and interconnected; second, other areas have been well covered in the companion essays in this volume. I would only add, though, that reforms in two other areas not covered in this book also need attention. The first is agriculture. The second is administrative reform, and the modernization of the decision-making structures of government. Space does not permit elaboration of the agenda for these two areas. As China demonstrated, a successful agriculture sector provides a strong base for industrial demand. India's agricultural policy framework is more than usually distorted, in part because jurisdiction falls between the center and the states. In this area, while the awareness of the issues is widespread, coordinated decision- making is proving difficult. By contrast, the issue of administrative reform is scarcely on the agenda, although there is general agreement that the existing structure does not permit the professionalism of policy making that India will increasingly require. I have also not dwelt on the large volume of action that needs to be taken at the level of individual states. What is encouraging is that states are increasingly competing with one another in the investment climate they can offer, while agreeing to limit ineffective fiscal incentives. Given this, poorly governed states are likely to increasingly lose out in the battle for private investment.

ISSUES OF IMPLEMENTATION

There is a widespread belief among the Indian elite that the reform agenda is well-established, that a consensus exists, and that the problems are ones of 'implementation'.

I believe this characterization to be false. In my view, the critical problem with India's reform program since 1991 has been the absence of overt political support for it, and the lack of a compelling political articulation of the necessity, indeed inevitability, of reform. Instead, reform has essentially been a technocratic project, although in the recently concluded elections, there were some signs of a greater political embrace by the Bharatiya Janata Party (BJP).

As a result of the political legwork that remains undone within parties, across parties and with the public at large, each issue needs to be fought over. I wish I could say that private industry is sufficiently united and enlightened to support reform wholeheartedly, but this degree of maturity is only slowly developing. The bureaucracy, an important player, remains divided, and dependent on political signals and leadership. Its great genius is to keep a rickety system functioning sufficiently to satisfy all claimants. It is not its role, and is beyond its capacity, to put together coalitions of potential beneficiaries. Unlike China, post-reform economic performance has not been so much better that it can create its own momentum. The shifts in Western sentiment towards globalization have not helped either.

But it is important not to be too pessimistic either. There has been little backsliding on the reforms of the 1990s. The rhetorical framework has been altered immeasurably. In lots of ways, India is a fundamentally different country from what it was in 1991. The rise of China shows what is possible even for a populous rural society, and presents both a challenge and a giant market at India's doorstep. India's software and business process outsourcing (BPO) successes as well as the successful negotiation of the Asian crisis have created confidence, though not complacency. The prevailing mood in Indian circles today is of challenge, but also of confidence for the medium term. In my view, that confidence is justified, provided India does the hard work that is necessary.

Comment

D. S. Brar
former Chief Executive Officer and Managing Director, Ranbaxy Laboratories Ltd.

India's economy in the past decade has excited the imagination of its citizens, as well as international policymakers, experts and observers. Nobody could have ignored the historical significance of a nation with a billion people-and more-attaining great advances in prosperity and modernity within a few decades. The destiny of the Indian economy offers exciting potential to the whole world; the challenge is to temper that thrill with realism.

Many macro indicators of the Indian economy have created a favorable impression globally, and most observers agree that this country has reached a growth threshold that is going to be higher than that of most other developing countries.

Yet, our own times teach us that all economic situations in the modern era are dynamic and often prone to rapid flux. The crises in the economies of countries, regions, and the world as a whole, that have occurred intermittently during the past two decades are ample testimony to this. So, it is important to look beyond numbers too. Any perspective to India's economic future has to be an intricate weave of physical projections, as well as the values, ideas and norms that are deployed.

This realization is also borne out by even the most cursory overview of what has happened in the Indian economy. From 1951 to 1981, India's GDP grew at 3.5 % annually, famously termed the 'Hindu rate'. Yet, per capita growth was only at 1.5% during this period. This phase also saw the institutionalization of the constrictive attitudes, policies and regulations that denuded the Indian economy of any sense of enterprise and competitiveness. Some efforts to break this mold were made in the next decade, 1981-91, wherein overall GDP grew at 5.6% annually, with per capita growth increasing at 3.4%. However, this growth, by and large, was funded by high external borrowings and deficit financing; and proved to be unsustainable by the end of the decade.

The next decade, 1991-2000, witnessed an overall 5.6% growth as well. Interestingly, if one disregards the crisis of the year 1991/92, the growth average for the other nine years was 6.1% (this actually shows that a short period of poor performance can affect the overall result). Per capita growth increased at 4%, marked by a newfound boom in consumer aspirations and national confidence.

Successive governments also took up wide-ranging economic reforms. Many manufacturing sectors successfully underwent the transition to higher efficiency and competitiveness. India's educated youth spearheaded the tremendous expansion in the services sector, as the world came to acknowledge their intelligent skills.

Yet, this growth has made the problem areas only more glaring. The latter include the abysmally slow pace of infrastructure development (barring telecommunications, to some extent), stagnation in agriculture, decay of our urban systems in the face of increasing demands of economic modernization, and an inertia in improving quality-of-life parameters. Thus, India had become one of the 10 fastest-growing economies in the world by the end of the decade, but it continued to rank below 110 or so countries in terms of the UNDP's Human Development Index.

There are three very basic lessons to be drawn from this experience, and these will be critical to the way India progresses and develops in the years to come. The first lesson is about investment. Any high and sustained growth would demand sustained high investment, and the Indian economy has not yet met this requirement. The government has to create initiatives that unleash far higher investment into various forms of production, ranging across infrastructure, manufacturing, and agriculture. These sectors contribute about 56.5% to the overall GDP, and 76% of total employment. The services sector contributes about 43.5% to the GDP and 24% of jobs, and has indeed been a key performer in the 1990s with 7-8% annual growth. However, the shortfall in the volume and quality of infrastructure (especially in power and transport), manufacturing output, and agricultural production dampens and constrains the overall economy.

Enhanced investment also encourages us to make the most of it. As a whole, India still uses its capital resources extremely inefficiently. A whole new paradigm of 'second-generation' reforms has to be put into place in this regard. For the infrastructure sector, this implies a regulatory environment that ensures optimal user charges, with subsidies (if at all) delivered only to those sections of society that really need them. The manufacturing sector requires holistic changes in the currently rigid labor laws, bankruptcy provisions, and 'reservations' for small-scale manufacturers. For the agriculture sector, this implies a complete unveiling of the terms of trade that will let farmers produce for the best prices anywhere, and not just for support prices announced by the government (the latter producing its own vicious financial cycle). Opening the doors of trade in agriculture will also create opportunities for new systems of agricultural storage, processing and distribution, which will further improve the returns on agricultural investments.

These issues are very basic not only for assuring remunerative returns on investment, they are critically required for any meaningful increase in the opportunities for employment in these sectors too. Again, a growth in manufacturing employment (from present levels of 16% of the total labor force) is the right mechanism to absorb surplus or under-used labor in the countryside (presently 60% of the total labor force). This, in turn, would ease the excruciating pressure of the population on land resources, as well as facilitate modern agricultural practices.

Second-generation reforms in the financial sector will also unlock the real potential of our foreign currency reserves, which have grown in recent times to cross the $100 billion threshold. We need policies that will ensure that these reserves are deployed towards generating a 'multiplier effect' on the overall economy. Such reforms also imply totally revamped and modern systems for capital flows within the country as well as internationally. Moreover, modern reform and practices in this regard will critically determine the extent to which we are able to pursue successful economic diplomacy in multilateral frameworks of trade and investment.

The second key lesson for growth relates to our population. India's government and policy planners believe in the imperative of planning and investing in the social sectors that are critical to the quality of life of the population. Yet, so much more needs to be done in this regard for our population in order for them to drive growth. Recent trends are worrying. It is evident in annual budgets, especially those of the state governments, that government spending, as a proportion of the total budget, on population control, health, nutrition, and education, is decreasing each year. Per capita spending on these sectors, too, compares unfavorably with most other emerging economies. This can be disastrous in view of the fact that investments in health and education have been key to the huge growth of the services sectors in recent times. If the tertiary sectors, especially the knowledge economy, are to grow further, new public-private partnerships must be created to improve public health and education.

Enhancements in social sector spending are even more critical in the areas of the environment, water and sanitation. In the Indian context, our perspective on water is especially important. There are contrasting views on whether we are blessed with adequate water, or whether we have too little of it. But everybody agrees that we use water inefficiently. If our standard of living is to grow, our manufacturing to be augmented, our agriculture to reach higher growth trajectories, we have to learn to use water productively, as it is a most vital resource, and create appropriate pricing and regulatory strategies for its use.

The third element for growth relates to the overall mindset with which we perceive our economic objectives, as well as the positioning of our people and nation in the world. India has already jettisoned the introverted mentality of a closed economy. But we are still on a learning curve as far as developing new civic norms and values that are essential to an open economy are concerned.

A new civic mindset would be all about transparency in mutual relations as well as with the outside world, upholding the rule of law in any given situation, and acknowledging universal values. Significantly, businessmen, industrialists and other creators of wealth will have to play a central role in this act. In the past, this group had been content to be at the periphery of civil society and national concerns. Now, they will have to create new public-private partnerships for the economy, the society, and the nation as a whole.

A clear focus on these three imperatives will add manifold value to whatever numbers we ascribe to India's economic future. It will create a seamless synchronicity between the rate of growth and its quality. India's infrastructure, agriculture, industry and services sectors will become arenas for a new generation of ideas that will take us towards modernity and advancement.

Interestingly, one of the outcomes of this scenario will be a new drive to build our cities, even as we improve the country's villages and agriculture. Throughout human history, great cities have been known to be cradles for civilization, as well as social and economic innovation and investment. Just imagine if Delhi, Mumbai, Bangalore, Hyderabad and a couple of others were to grow into truly modern global cities with world-class civic and economic infrastructure during our own times. The numbers related to investment and wealth as well as overall economic achievement of such a dream are gigantic. So is the scale of new civic sensibilities, new practices of democratic governance, and socio-economic organization that would be required.

Yet, the scenario indicates the real challenge for India. The economic drive in the last years of the 20th century saw us displaying comparatively rustic energies, which enabled us to burst through the proverbial cocoon. This effort must be reinvigorated and charged with much greater energy in the 21st century.

FINANCIAL REFORMS

Scenario

Alfred R. Berkeley III
Vice-Chairman, NASDAQ

The magic of India's opportunity lies in its ability to learn from the mistakes and the successes of other countries that have climbed the economic development ladder before it.

Understanding the patterns of increased use of various goods and services as incomes increased in the West has lowered the risks of venture capitalists investing in India. Likewise, the Indian government draws lessons from the successes and failures of various public policies in countries whose economies have earlier grown large. This rather extraordinary ability to see glimpses of the future in the history of others can, and should, be very useful.

At the risk of seeming a naive outside observer, let me suggest a few of the big lessons learned by others that might be useful to India.

The single most fundamental lesson to learn is to encourage private savings, broadly and deeply, in the economy. The currency must be reliable, and inflation is the enemy of reliability. A series of laws must be enacted to make ownership, transfer of ownership and bankruptcy reliable. Since ownership is the key to savings, savings the key to capital formation, and capital formation the key to prosperity and economic development, properly set-out laws on ownership is an essential foundation. Having a clear deed to the land is the bedrock of property rights, which enable the existence of credit. Credit is the 'force multiplier' of capital formation.

Upon the foundation of proper laws about ownership, a speedy judiciary can make the rule of law meaningful. India's courts are too slow and justice delayed is justice denied. The United States was able to create a stable civil society because wave upon wave of penniless immigrants were able to become owners of the productive assets of the American economy. First, it was through America's Homestead Acts, which conveyed clear, durable titles to land.

In modern America, the relatively wide use of stock options and employee ownership plans have given millions of Americans both a vested interest in a stable society and the motivation to work hard to build the company where they are employee-owners. America began to accumulate significant risk capital when it passed legislation protecting employee retirement savings and encouraging incremental voluntary savings through tax-advantaged individual retirement plans owned and directed by the savers.

While there is no doubt that the United States has several policies that work against capital formation, on balance, capital formation has increased since America moved decisively towards equity ownership in the 1970s. The specific steps taken at the time were first, the reduction of taxes on capital gains from 50% to 28%, and then to 20%; second, the passage of the Employee Retirement Income Security Act, which is important because it permitted pension trustees to invest a portion of their assets in venture capital; third, the development of tax-advantaged individual retirement plans; and fourth, the creation of the NASDAQ Stock Market, which gave young entrepreneurial companies access to public markets. India should create strong incentives to spread ownership broadly and deeply.

Romania offers an interesting lesson for India in the realm of privatization. India is privatizing, though not in the way that Romania had done when the latter privatized all its old communist state-owned enterprises. Romania did not try to sell the enterprise in the open market nor to strategic buyers. Instead, Romania gave shares to every citizen.

India should do the same. It could either distribute shares individually or as a 'mutual fund' of all privatized companies. The shares would be traded in the open market and private capital ownership would be widely dispersed.

Private, instead of government-run, pensions should be encouraged and they should be well-regulated and transparent. A large percentage of the capital formed by retirement savings in the U.S. is available to support risk equity. In contrast, in France, where most pensions are held by the government, capital is not available to support competitive free enterprises. France has lost much of its relative economic strength as a result of compounding over a period of 60 years following WWII.

This has punished pensions invested in government bonds as opposed to pensions invested in the equities of competitive businesses. India need not commit this mistake.

While it is not well understood, much of America's current job losses to outsourcing are a result of the American tax structure. America taxes its most productive corporations for earnings made anywhere in the world, and also taxes capital gains. Governments should tax consumption, not capital, and should not drive away (but rather, attract) corporations that are within their jurisdictions by taxing the earnings these corporations made in other jurisdictions.

One of the most interesting challenges India faces is the possibility of juggling the federal bureaucracies' tendency to control everything and the states' need for more autonomy to innovate. Shifting decision-making authority towards the states and away from the national bureaucracy raj would undoubtedly spur innovation. Regional competition among states would likely be a good thing, and like compound interest, would show many benefits over time.

The hard lessons that the United States had learned over time as regards patents and intellectual property are another area that India can learn from. For years, the United States believed that ideas developed with public dollars belonged to everybody. We missed, of course, the most basic lesson of human nature which was that anything owned by everybody is owned by nobody. We eventually realized that invention was only a tiny percentage of the total cost of converting an invention into a product and a product into a business. We determined, through the Bayh-Dole Act, to permit inventions that had been developed with federal funds to be licensed with good titles and exclusivity to for-profit companies. We have seen hundreds of new products and businesses created as a result.

The Indian patent system is currently designed to permit Indian companies to invent around someone else's patent and avoid paying for it. This may feel good politically in the short run, but it will hurt India in the long run. It is just another part of the issue of clear titles, and is every bit as applicable to intellectual property as it is to real estate.

Research and development in India could be accelerated if India learns the lessons revealed in the U.S. and Europe. Research and development funds could be set aside for the many who are employees of national or state institutes, laboratories and universities. In the U.S., particularly in the universities, scientists must compete for research grants. While this system has many problems, it does achieve the Darwinian goal of forcing tough competition among the scientists. Professors who cannot win grants to cover their work often lose their labs. Of course this is painful in the specific, but again, like compounding interest, is beneficial to the overall economy as time goes by.

Insurance is another area of opportunity for India. Pooling risks has been one of the principal tools of economic growth in the West. India should learn from the problems in the United States, particularly in the field of medical insurance.

America made a mistake just after WWII in allowing health insurance to be a corporate deduction. The result has been a massive consolidation of power in the hands of health insurers, whose interests in reducing costs happen to parallel the interest of the corporation-employer to reduce costs. With both the insurance company and his employer lined up against him, and without a vibrant, viable alternative to the employer-purchased health insurance, the poor citizen is left with almost no role in the purchase decision, and with no advocate.

America would be far better off if, like automobile insurance, individuals bought their own insurance and had options to switch in an open market. Everyone would be better off were there less concentration in the health insurance market.

Changing the status quo or integrating change into the political process is undoubtedly difficult. But India need not repeat the mistakes of others who had similarly faced the problems of growth. India is clearly 'on the move', and can reach its potential through smart public policy. Public policy matters, and simple concepts of private property, clear title and ownership rights can go a long way towards giving India the economic ideal of widely dispersed ownership of productive assets which will lead to a stable civil society and vibrant growth.

Comment

P. Chidambaram
Minister of Finance, India

INTRODUCTION

In the last 20 years, India had transformed itself not once but twice. The first transformation was between 1984 and 1991 when a new generation of political leaders came to the fore and assumed office. An old political party which had reinvented itself rose to become the principal opposition. A clutch of regional parties representing the lower-class of India laid claim to power. Few have reflected upon the profound change that these developments had brought to India.

1991 marked, of course, the beginning of another major transformation of India. The change was forced upon India by external factors. India reformed because it was compelled to reform. India has changed, otherwise the country would have defaulted on its international obligations and brought the economy to ruin. Since then, of course, reform has become a part of India's political vocabulary, part of India's political discourse. Today, more political parties and more sections of the people willingly embrace reforms.

India today is an opportunity. For the first time, India is clearly riding a wave of sustained economic growth. In the 12 years that I have been witness to the economic reform, there is always the fear that if we took two steps forward we may be forced to take a step backward. India has had three good years of growth and then there was a danger of slipping. India has had again two years of growth and then we fell behind for another couple of years.

For the first time, there is universal acceptance of the fact that India now rides the crest of the waves, and this wave could sustain economic reforms and growth for at least another 10 years. While India's present average growth rate is close to 6.5%, what it needs is a sustained growth of at least 7 or 8%.

Today, it is universally accepted that India is poised to begin a 10-year period of sustained growth. Why has this come about? It has come about because of increasing consensus on the economic reforms. Let me list the matters where there have been broad consensus.

Fiscal Prudence and Discipline

First, there is consensus on the view that we must observe fiscal prudence and fiscal discipline. There are very few voices which speak of spending one's way to prosperity. In 2003, the parliament of India enacted the Fiscal Responsibility and Management Act. In 2005, after the new government assumed office on 5 July, I endorsed that act. That act is a great discipliner. As long as that act remains in the statute book, and it will do so for another 10 years, it will require every government and every finance minister to reduce the fiscal deficit and the revenue deficit year after year until the revenue deficit is wiped out in 2008/09. On fiscal prudence and fiscal discipline, there is today a very broad consensus.

Trade

The second area of consensus is that trade, even if it means a large trade deficit, is beneficial. I remember in 1991 when I was commerce minister and the merchandized trade deficit crossed \$3 billion. There were prophets of doom who said that opening up exports and imports would lead India to disaster.

Today, a \$12 billion-deficit does not even raise an eyebrow. No one asked whether we had more imports than exports. Everyone accepts that even if imports are growing faster than exports, both are good for India. Our exports are currently growing by 24% in dollar terms; our imports by 37% in dollar terms.

When India's trade with China expands, when the free trade arrangement with Thailand, Singapore and the ASEAN are rolled out to their full potential, India will once again become a major trading country. There is broad consensus that trade is a great driver of growth and that trade, even if it results in trade deficit, is beneficial to India.

External Management

Another area of consensus is that India must manage the external front very carefully—that external debts are carefully managed; that external commercial borrowing is carefully managed; and that the flow of funds into India is carefully monitored. Unless there is very prudent and wise management of the external sector, the kind of shocks that some Asian nations underwent could hit India and other countries some day in the future. Broad consensus on external management has resulted in $127 billion in India's reserves today. That is 127 times more than the reserves in 1991. The external debt is only $112 billion. The short-term debt is a very small proportion of the external debt.

As reserves pour into India, the Indian government is carefully watching the quality of these reserves. Are they foreign direct investment? Are they foreign institutional investment? Are they from hedged funds? Are they debt-creating flows or non-debt creating flows? Are they remittances from Indians who live abroad? There is a broad consensus that if we manage the external economy well, we will only become stronger every year and that is what has happened over the past 12 years.

Investment Promotion

There is also consensus that we must promote investment. The state alone cannot find funds for investment. Once upon a time, it was believed that the state will raise the funds, the state will invest the funds and the state will be the driver of economic growth. Fortunately, that perspective no longer prevails. We now welcome investments into every sector of India's economy, not only manufacturing or industry or services, but also, what is more important, agriculture.

In the last few years, India has realized that there is a broad consensus on agriculture as requiring, perhaps, the greatest quantity of investment. It is agriculture which requires the best technology and the best practices. It is agriculture which requires new markets. It is agriculture which requires new inputs, new seeds, new fertilizers, new pesticides, new technology, new post-harvest practices, new transport chains, new opportunities to export and new markets. That is why we welcome today foreign investment in agriculture. We have a foreign company helping us to grow tomatoes in India. Another foreign consultant helps the state of West Bengal grow potatoes. Contract farming has become a very common practice. Agriculture exports are likely to double every year for the next 10 years.

OPPORTUNITIES FOR INVESTMENT

All this shows the long distance that has been traveled. But still, the full benefits of the great opportunity that is called India have not been reaped. No other country requires such a vast quantity of investment in power, in telecommunications, in roads, in airports, in sea ports, in petroleum, and in refineries, in virtually every sphere of economic activity.

In telecommunications, India needs $40 billion; and in power, $12 billion every year for the next 10-15 years. 13,146 kilometers of road will be constructed and that will require $13 billion. At least six world-class airports and 20 others will be built along India's long coastline. There are petroleum and gas reserves to be explored onshore and offshore. Steel capacities are to be trebled. The huge mineral wealth that lies beneath our land in the states of Bihar, Bengal, Orissa and elsewhere have yet to be exploited.

All this requires vast amounts of money. It is the business of the Indian government to ensure that the environment remains enabling, investor-friendly, helpful and one where investors can make profits. For many years, the government has created this enabling environment. But while the government sometimes speaks the language of business, sometimes it does not. This has to change.

Therefore, an investment commission has been set up. It acts as a conduit between business and government. The three-member commission consists of Chairman Ratan Tata, the doyen of Indian business; Mr Deepak Parekh, a well-known international banker; and Dr Ashok Ganguly, an internationally-known businessman.

With the full authority of the government, the three-member commission will engage business in India and elsewhere in the world, hold discussions with investors and invite them to invest in India. It will be the government's face and voice in interactions with investors. It will listen to investors, understand their problems and identify opportunities for them. It will advise the government on what needs to be done in order to attract more investments into India.

With this investment commission, India will make tremendous progress in attracting larger and larger quantities of investment. The goal set by the prime minister is $150 billion over the next 10 years.

The present government has brought about many improvements. When it assumed office, it inherited an industrial growth rate which was 6.2%. In the first half of 2005, it was 7.9%. Manufacturing has grown by 8.2%, electricity by 7.7% and mining by 4.9%. Initially, sensex was 5399 and on the day of the budget, it was 4843; it recently hit 6323, the highest in the history of the stock exchange. The rupee was Rs45.12 to the dollar; today, it is Rs44.01 to the dollar. Our reserves stood at $118 billion; today, it stands at $127 billion. In 2004, Indian business went to the market on 15 occasions in the first half of the year and raised a little less than $500 million. This year, in 25 issues, they have raised over $3 billion so far. Credit to industry, services and agriculture in 2004 was about $10 billion. Over the same period in 2005, it rose to $22 billion.

CONCLUSION

India is growing. India is growing at a brisk pace. The opportunities are growing. The opportunities are growing at an enormous rate and businesses must seize the opportunity. The Indian government will do its part to help. India aims to take her rightful place as a nation where the creation of wealth is celebrated, as a nation where the creation of wealth leads to the creation of jobs and greater income, and where wealth can be shared among a billion people.

But India has its problems. These problems are related to rural India, to problems of poverty and disease, and the lack of potable water, proper sanitation, shortage of schools and medical dispensaries. However, there is confidence that the government, public revenues and public administration can be brought together to address these problems.

India presents many opportunities. The country is expected to be the fourth-largest economy in the world in the next few years. India wants to be a large economy because they have a large people and the needs of this people are great. These needs can only be met if the country grows and progresses, if the country can create wealth for all. I am confident that in the next 10 years, as all sectors work together, the Indian economy can grow at not less than 7% a year. When business and government work hand in hand, this growth rate can be sustained consistently for the next decade and decades after. This decade of opportunity may turn out to be India's most promising decade.

Comment

K. V. Kamath
Chief Executive Officer and Managing Director, ICICI Bank Limited

2004 has proven to be one of the best years ever for the Indian economy. All three sectors of the economy—services, industry and agriculture—have recorded robust growth rates. Foreign exchange reserves reached new highs, strengthening the economy's resilience to externalities. Inflation and interest rates were stable, and capital markets were buoyant, creating a platform for heightened economic activity. The figure of 8% growth in GDP, which used to be a matter of conjecture for economists and strategists not so long ago, is now a reality.

STRONG FUNDAMENTALS AND SUSTAINABLE GROWTH

The economic scenario that we see today is the outcome of a decade of economic reform. The opening-up of the economy to greater private participation and integration with the global markets has brought to the fore the entrepreneurial ability and knowledge capital latent in the Indian people. This has caused a deep structural change in the economy, the most visible aspect of which is the rapid growth of the services sector.

Knowledge has emerged as the key driver of our economy today. The share of information technology and software services in India's exports has grown from 5% to 20% in six years.

Yet the sustainability of this growth continues to be questioned in some quarters. Academics appear to be biased towards manufacturing-led growth—large capital investments and increases in bank loans to industry, creation of industrial capacity and employment of people in factories.

What they ignore is that the knowledge economy has established a completely new growth paradigm. It sublimates the entire process of wealth creation to directly leverage human capital and build economic value. It does not require large capital investments or bank credit; the cost of creating a job in a business process outsourcing facility would be approximately one-tenth, or perhaps less, than the cost of creating a job in the manufacturing sector. It is therefore important to understand that this is a new economic reality, which draws its sustenance from the power and momentum that the Indian people provide.

The services sector will continue to be the key driver of growth. The knowledge economy and the favorable demographic profile, with 69% of the population being less than 35 years of age, will spur consumption demand. The growth of the services sector has increased the economic output of other sectors as well. We are already seeing the beginning of the release of pent-up demand for key personal needs—housing, consumer durables, automobiles and two-wheelers, affordable and accessible financial services. This trend will gather momentum with the passage of time.

The other principal driver of growth will be infrastructure building. There has indeed been significant success in some areas—initiatives in telecommunications have led to a rapid increase in the telephone subscriber base and an equally rapid rationalization of pricing, achieving the twin objectives of growth and affordability.

The national roads development program is also proving to be very successful. The challenge is to replicate this across other sectors like power and urban infrastructure. This will improve the quality of life of the people and increase participation in economic activity, with immense long-term benefits for the economy.

The growth in manufacturing will take off from the growth in both services and infrastructure. Both these sectors will spur demand for the output of the manufacturing sector. The other major driver of growth in the manufacturing sector will be exports. After a prolonged and often painful period of restructuring and repositioning, the Indian manufacturing sector is now proving it can compete globally on cost and quality. From becoming key suppliers to some of the world's largest corporations to setting up manufacturing and distribution bases overseas, Indian industrial companies have truly come of age.

To sum up, with an efficient economic paradigm, India is well-positioned to achieve robust growth in the coming years. This growth is not being achieved by pump-priming or large-scale debt-financed capital formation; it is being achieved by leveraging the knowledge advantage, and by improving competitiveness and viability in traditional areas of the economy.

THE FUTURE OF INDIAN BANKING

The future of the banking sector is, of course, rooted in this economic scenario. The evolution of the Indian financial sector has mirrored the transformation of the Indian economy.

A decade ago, the financial sector was almost entirely state-owned; today, the private sector has a sizeable market share even in life insurance—a government monopoly that was opened to private participation just a few years ago.

Financial intermediaries functioned in separate silos, with a narrow breadth of products and operations; today, there are financial supermarkets that offer their customers a range of products under one umbrella. But how well-prepared is India to meet the challenge of global competition? To answer this question, it is important to address a few key issues.

The Myth of High Intermediation Costs

The supposedly high intermediation costs and low efficiency of Indian banks is a matter of frequent discussion. What this approach ignores is the low ticket size of banking relationships and transactions in India vis-à-vis other economies, though the number of banking accounts and the transaction volumes are comparable. India today has about 450 million deposit accounts—but with an average retail deposit account size of only about US$450.

Thus, an Indian bank with the same number of customer accounts and therefore approximately the same number of transactions as an international bank has a much smaller balance sheet size than the international bank. The comparison of intermediation costs relative to business volumes therefore does not present the correct perspective.

A more meaningful insight into the relative levels of intermediation costs of Indian and international banks is provided by the analysis of the operating cost per customer transaction. This gives a different picture.

For instance, an internal benchmarking study undertaken by ICICI Bank shows that its annual technology operating expenditure per customer transaction is between 5% and 10% of the expenditure levels of a range of international banks, from the United States to Australia.

This high-volume, low ticket size scenario is one of the primary reasons for the large number of branches and the over-manning witnessed in older Indian banks, primarily in the public sector. Thus, the key challenge for banks is to manage a large number of low-value relationships and a large volume of transactions efficiently. This can only be achieved through the use of technology.

At the same time, as the economy grows and per capita economic indicators improve, the size of banking customer relationships will also increase. As bank balance sheets will grow through enhancement of existing customer account values, banks will not need to add brick-and-mortar channels or manpower to handle larger transaction volumes to support this growth. Thus, the same level of capital and operating expenditure will be leveraged to a far greater extent. This will be a key driver of the growth and improvement in profitability of the banking sector in India.

Technology

Technology is a focus area for the entire banking sector in India today. Older-generation banks that relied on brick-and-mortar channels and large workforces have realized that embracing technology is critical to competing and surviving in this business. The pace of adoption of technology in the large public sector banks has accelerated in recent times. Most banks have an articulated technology strategy.

While aggressively investing in technology, banks have not lost sight of the need to leverage technology optimally. Agreements among several banks to share their ATM networks are a case in point. This has offered enhanced convenience to the customers of the banking system without duplicating investment or creating ‘over-capacity’.

Technology addresses the risks and inefficiencies inherent in a banking model dependent on physically-manned delivery channels with high degrees of manual intervention in processing and service delivery.

At the same time, technology brings with it its own set of challenges and risks. Constraints of time and distance vanish with technology. Banks need to build capabilities to deal with this. The core banking solution can itself pose a risk; a failure or interruption in its operations can severely impair the functioning of the bank. Banks must therefore be alive to the complexities and challenges that technology poses as they harness technology in their businesses.

Asset Quality

Asset quality in the Indian banking system was impacted by the challenges that liberalization posed for industrial units set up under protectionist regimes. Asset quality was also affected by the increasing exposure of the economy to global competition and volatility in the global economy, especially in the commodity sectors. Banks had significant concentrations in their lendings to these sectors. This issue has now been addressed by several positive developments.

Banks have been aggressive in asset resolution, both in terms of recoveries and restructuring of debt, and in terms of higher provisions to cushion their balance sheets against potential losses.

The regulatory and legal framework has been supportive, with legislation to facilitate recovery and asset reconstruction, and regulatory initiatives on corporate debt restructuring. The turnaround in the industrial sector and the resurgence of Indian manufacturing has improved the financial position of borrowers and positively impacted the quality of bank assets. The efficiency focus and international competitiveness of Indian industry has positive implications for incremental credit risk.

At the same time, the growth of the retail credit market has provided an opportunity for banks which had so far been dependent primarily on the industrial sector as a customer for credit products. They can now diversify and de-risk their balance sheets.

Regulatory Framework

The Indian regulatory framework has also evolved as India opens up to the world. The financial system has become increasingly sophisticated and complex and the financial regulatory framework is comparable internationally. The legal framework is also being addressed, by the enactment of enabling legislation that provides a legal basis for new facets of banking and the streamlining of recovery procedures. Considerable progress has been made in liberalizing foreign investment in the sector, whether in terms of strategic investments or expansion of operations by foreign banks or investments by financial investors. This regulatory framework provides a sound basis for further opening up the banking sector and giving banks the opportunity to expand the scope of their operations.

The Indian banking sector is thus well-positioned on these key issues and is geared to meet the competitive challenge posed by globalization.

CONCLUSION

The Indian economy as a whole and the Indian banking sector are today characterized by the same mood of confidence and optimism. This is based on strong underlying fundamentals. The continuing growth of the services sector and the knowledge economy will drive wealth creation and income growth. This, coupled with a favorable demographic position, will fuel demand for goods and services.

For banks, this will not only mean an increase in demand for banking products but also an increase in customer relationship sizes, resulting in further leveraging of the already-competitive cost of intermediation. Infrastructure development will provide a further catalyst for growth. The manufacturing sector will benefit not only from a growing domestic demand but also from a growing external orientation and a demonstrated ability to leverage India's resources and cost structure to compete globally.

The banking system has addressed the legacy asset quality issues and a sound regulatory framework has been established. The banking sector has created a robust platform for leveraging opportunities and meeting competitive challenges.

GEOPOLITICS

Scenario

Sundeep Waslekar
President, Strategic Foresight Group

India has entered a period of uncertainty. India's business environment in the next decade is expected to be influenced as much by external geopolitical factors, as by the country's initiatives in the area of economic, social, political and judicial reforms.

While reforms are very much within the realm of choices that India can make, it is necessary to examine if and to what extent India can influence the emerging geopolitical outlook. The developments that would shape this outlook may not necessarily be easily determined based on an analysis of present trends. They are more likely to be a series of discontinuities, therefore, there is a need to identify key uncertainties. In order to do this, one needs to take a view that transcends the traditional India-Pakistan prism and consider broader developments that may have an impact on India's geopolitical outlook.

India's geopolitical needs have to be examined in a world order where the United States has supremacy in military ideology and economy; NATO is the predominant military coalition in the world; democracy is at least notionally accepted as the universal ideology of governance; the free market is the dominant instrument of conducting economic relations; and technology is the greatest driver of economic growth.

It is a paradigm where elite societies seek to maintain security in a disorderly and volatile world, where regional powers such as China, Russia and Iran seek to protect their sovereignty and influence. Constructive non-state actors such as NGOs, as well as destructive non-state actors, such as terrorist groups, are challenging the present economic and political structure. The way that these groups are managed in the next few years will be a key determinant of the geopolitical outlook, not just for India, but also for the whole world.

We are in a phase in history where the new rules of conduct of international relations are being framed with the doctrine of pre-emption, subordination of sovereignty and primacy of prosperity. The nation-state remains the primary principle for organizing societies, though it is increasingly being challenged by forces within and outside its control. Economics and information have emerged, in addition to the military, as the main currencies of power.

It is an era where the theater of primary geopolitical action has shifted from Europe to Asia, an era in which developments in Pakistan, Central and West Asia, and China will determine India's geopolitical outlook more than its immediate neighbours in South Asia. These events provide India with both a challenge and an opportunity to influence the shape of the decade to come. The manner in which India makes decisions relating to its foreign policy and strategic neighborhood will determine its future.

FOUR SCENARIOS

Four scenarios comprising alternative policy mixes that India may choose within the framework of directions set by identified drivers are developed. These include American ambitions in Asia, internal dynamics in West Asian countries, China's economic resurgence, polarization in Pakistan, risk of a war over water between India and Pakistan, changing approach to international relations, and economic disparities within the country.

The policy mix chosen by India will very much depend on the vision of the country. From 1950 to 1990, India had a vision of itself as a self-reliant, non-aligned, secular state, albeit disregarding its economic potential. From 1991 to 2001, India viewed itself as a globalizing economy, but an increasingly fractious society. From 2002 to 2020, India would like to see itself transform from a developing to a developed country.

There are four possible scenarios for India's geopolitical outlook for the future. The first compares India to a *Frog in the Pond*, who looks at the sky above him, muses about it, but is essentially focused on the pond that he lives in. India looks at the big wide world, muses about its permanent membership at the UN Security Council, but conducts its geopolitics very much from an Indian-Pakistani prism. The domestic ramification of this is that it favors a development strategy, which benefits the top 20%—really 2%—of the people, ignoring the vast Indian population.

In this scenario, U.S. Secretary of State, EU officials, Chinese and Japanese leaders regularly visit India but they want to discuss strategic stability in South Asia and the resumption of India-Pakistan talks. They do not consider it relevant to engage India in core decisions on global issues, except as a courtesy.

On the other hand, India maintains normal relations with China and Iran, mostly in trade, but does not consider nurturing strategic relations with these countries as a bargaining chip in its negotiations with the U.S. and EU.

In economics, India is known as the cost-effective supplier of IT services. In 2010, she earns US$50 billion in exports, but employs only a little over 1 million professionals. India is still not seen as a large market but merely a supplier of cheap factors of production.

The second scenario is that of the *Cobra in the Hole*. Like a cobra which is secure in its own dwelling, and is not concerned about the outside world, except for the prey that he surreptitiously grabs and eats in the security of his own home, India decides to adopt an inward-looking mold. It focuses on domestic growth and stability. It does not want to have any negotiation with other countries on any issue, except where it is almost essential and when it is seeking an occasional export opportunity to bolster its exchange reserves.

In this scenario, the government elected in 2004 decides to put its own house in order through a domestic economic revival. It announces tough carrot-and-stick approaches to deal with terrorism, crime, and other law and order issues.

Foreign policy is managed by the professional foreign office. India's participation in SAARC is nominal. The president represents the country at SAARC government summits from 2004 to 2009.

Meanwhile, Pakistan continues to discuss Kashmir. India makes it clear that it will have no talks with Pakistan on this or any other issue. It strengthens defense forces on the border to pre-empt any Pakistani attack and gives security agencies a free hand to deal with terrorists in a brutal manner. India abrogates Article 370 in Jammu and Kashmir.

India is least bothered about the tumultuous changes in China and the Middle East. It introduces stiff conservation measures to ensure its energy security and encourages companies to invest in local oil and gas fields. India accedes to all the global economic and environmental treaties but refuses to accede to any security treaty. It also restricts the entry of international human rights organizations and the media to the country. In order to protect itself from global uncertainty and irrational Pakistan, India advances its nuclear weapons and missile program, against global criticism.

The third scenario is that of a *Calf in the Shadow* of its mother, depending on the latter for food and security. Here, India joins U.S.-led Western alliance and agrees to toe the line without question. New governments in Washington and New Delhi decide to enter into a security pact in view of the nearing collapse of Pakistan and strong sense of insecurity all over South Asia.

India offers independence to the Kashmir valley under U.S. advice, and against domestic protests. FBI is put in service to assist the central government to control opposition at home. The World Bank and other multilateral organizations offer India a huge amount of long-term soft loans to develop urban infrastructure, power, and education. All restrictions on foreign trade and investments are lifted. The rupee is convertible on the capital account. India restricts its dialogue with Russia, China and Iran to economic and technical issues.

The politicians with a rural base have very little access to the prime minister who spends most of his time on foreign policy issues. The opposition also takes a leaf from the book of the ruling party and their leaders cultivate senate staffers and academics in Washington.

India's growth rate goes up to 8%, exports increase and a sense of prosperity arrives in the country by 2010. There are protests in rural areas against growing disparities, but the government manages cohesion by corruption and terrorism by counter-terrorism. Between 2006 and 2010, the biggest problem is terrorism. India now not only attracts terrorist attacks on its own account, but also for being an ally of the Western coalition.

The fourth scenario is that of the *Lion in the Emblem* (the three-faced lion in India's national emblem), which believes in the victory of principles, and confidently perceives the whole world in all directions. Similarly, India re-formulates its geopolitical vision with confidence and commitment to certain principles.

Economic growth at a consistent 9% growth rate is the top priority. Moreover, it is to be achieved by widening the base of the domestic economy to create a sense of belonging to the state among all sections of society. There is a sustained effort to transform the agrarian economy into a productive, well-respected sector, creating employment with high returns for millions of new entrants in the rural labor market. There is substantial decline in youth propensity for crime and terrorism.

At the same time, there is a sustained effort to improve the technological edge of the economy by shifting the focus of the IT sector from maintenance to product development, and by developing biotechnology in both pharmaceuticals and agriculture.

India launches Resolution, Reconciliation and Reconstruction initiatives in Jammu and Kashmir, the northeastern states and Naxalite-affected parts of central and northern India. Preventive measures are introduced in eastern Gujarat, Bihar and UP. All political parties emphasize genuine secularism and enter into an all-party accord to refrain from using caste and communal cards for electoral purposes.

India develops close relations with Europe, Russia, Iran, China and the U.S., and asserts its right to have independent relations with other countries. In 2006, Indian diplomacy launches an initiative for a new world order, with a Marshall Fund-type global transfer mechanism to reduce gaps in resources and know-how. India gathers the support of Russia, China and West Asian countries for this proposal. In 2009, the new U.S. administration endorses these ideas. In 2012, new institutions are created. In 2015, India is in the top bracket of the World Competitiveness Index. G-8, which had become G-9 with the inclusion of China in 2010, is made G-10 in 2015. India is its new member.

CONCLUSION

Each of the four scenarios has its advantages and disadvantages. India must decide which mix of advantages and disadvantages would be in its best interest.

- *Frog in the Pond* - narrow domestic growth, low external openness
- *Cobra in the Hole* - wide internal growth, low external openness
- *Calf in the Shadow* - narrow domestic growth, wide external openness
- *Lion in the Emblem* - wide internal growth, wide external openness

Of the four scenarios, *Cobra in the Hole* and *Calf in the Shadow* are not impossible, especially over the next 20 years, as it is difficult to predict how the Indian society will change, but they are least likely if assessed by the barometer of realities at the end of 2003.

The most plausible scenarios are *Frog in the Pond* and *Lion in the Emblem*. It is therefore essentially a Frog and Lion show! Both require hard choices not only in security and foreign policies, but also in the domestic political, social and economic agenda.

In making the choices, it is necessary to consider key certainties and uncertainties. Key certainties are:

- India's long-term strategic value;
- India's short-term perception of Pakistan vis-à-vis a problem child;
- Changes in Iran and other West Asian countries;
- China's emergence as a center of global industrial production;
- The spread of terrorism; and,
- The primacy of technology and economic advancement over sovereignty.

Key uncertainties are:

- Turbulence in the Middle East and energy markets;
- Turbulence in China and Korean peninsula; and,
- Collapse of Pakistan and temptation to use nuclear weapons.

Whatever the choice, it would be in India's interest to formulate a well-considered view whether it wants to be a frog, cobra, calf or lion. And then it would be necessary to take the required steps to convert that view into a reality.

Comment

Natwar Singh
Minister for Foreign Affairs, India

Dr. Henry Kissinger predicted a few years ago that the future world would have six poles—America, Japan, China, Russia, the European Union, and India. If we take away America, which, in any case, is the pre-eminent power in the world, all the other countries belong to either Europe or Asia. Thus, the future history of the world will be largely determined by the interplay of relations between Europe and Asia.

India's ex-president Jawaharlal Nehru was prescient enough to have seen this as early as in 1951. He said, "Asia has a very long history behind it and for long ages, it has played an outstanding part in the world. Its emergence from colonial status is making a great difference to the balance of forces in the world. The old equilibrium has been upset and can never be restored… Therefore... it is of the utmost importance that Europe and Asia should understand each other."

ON ASIA

Jawaharlal Nehru once described Asia as "the mother of continents and the cradle of history's major civilizations". Today, Asia is the continent where two-thirds of the world's population reside. The debate on whether the 21st century belongs to Asia or not is an ongoing one, but there is no denying the fact that Asia is poised to play a significant role in international relations. Asia is now the center of economic growth and commercial dynamism. It has the world's most youthful populations. Asia is the fastest growing continent, with China and India set to emerge as the world's second- and third-largest economies over the next few decades.

Yet the region is also prone to instability from national strategic rivalries, economic and political transitions, and rapid social transformations. Hence, the emergence of Asia is in reality the sum of the success of each of its parts. The economic dynamism of Asia will be sustained by growing connectivity and infrastructure development. It will also be reinforced by the evident emphasis on integrating markets through free trade arrangements, restructuring and reforms in individual economies.

Asia is also the principal source of the world's energy supply. There are ever new and impressive discoveries of oil and gas not only in the Persian Gulf region but also in India, Bangladesh, Myanmar, Indonesia and Vietnam. China sits on foreign exchange reserves of nearly $300 billion. India, on the other hand, is emerging as the major hub of international technology products and services. India's foreign exchange reserves have crossed the $120 billion mark and exports have recorded a steady growth of 10% in recent years. Some of the smaller countries like Vietnam and Thailand are also growing very fast, at rates of more than 6%.

Nehru's vision of a resurgent Asia and India's critical engagement in reshaping its destiny was based on three basic assumptions. First, that India was geo-strategically central to Asia, for being "so situated as to be the meeting point of western and northern, and eastern and southeastern Asia." Secondly, its historical and cultural roots were deeply embedded into the larger evolution of Asia over the centuries. Nehru was acutely conscious of these roots when he said, "If you should know India, you have to go to Afghanistan and Western Asia, to Central Asia, to China and Japan and to the countries of South Asia." The third assumption underlying Nehru's approach to Asia was that the decolonized and newly independent Asian countries would like to keep off from great power rivalries and conflicts, and also free themselves forever from political and economic bondage. In this freedom, Nehru saw a constructive and decisive possibility of Asia lending its legitimate weight in world politics in favor of peace and stability. But for this, Asian solidarity was a precondition and India was willing to work for it. In so doing, Nehru also underlined the roles of regionalism and institutionalization of cooperation and mutual understanding.

ON EUROPE

Today, the European Union has become virtually synonymous with Europe. The recent developments in the EU are of great importance to the world community. The bold and dynamic steps taken by the EU such as the Enlargement, the EU Constitution and the euro have enabled the EU to carve out for itself a distinct personality. With the accession of 10 new member states, in terms of population, the EU has become bigger than NAFTA, with a combined population of over 450 million. By the time the EU enlargement process reaches conclusion, the EU's borders will extend from Belarus to the Black Sea to Iraq, increasing the EU's population by 50%. But the process is not going to be easy. Europe is deeply divided, for instance, on the issue of Turkey's accession to the EU. If Turkey is admitted, it will mean the entry of the first Muslim country into the EU. If it is not, the EU will be perceived as an exclusively Christian club. The enlargement of the European Union will, therefore, not only have a profound effect on the world, but also on Europe itself.

ON EUROPE-ASIA PARTNERSHIP

There can thus be no doubt that both Asia and Europe have to work together. The question before us is, how will the partnership between Asia and Europe unfold? As the elections in India and the more recent ones in the U.S. have shown, crystal gazing is a rather hazardous occupation. Nevertheless, I feel that there are sufficient pointers for us to outline the dynamics which will shape the partnership between Asia and Europe in the first quarter of the 21st century.

On the political side, I think both Asia and Europe have a shared interest in strengthening multilateralism. The developments in Iraq have reiterated the need for effective multilateralism. The EU will continue to seek external support for strengthening multilateralism, and countries like India and China and the regional blocs such as ASEAN are increasingly seen as promoters of this idea.

The debate on the relevance of the UN in the 21st century assumes significance in this context. Both Asia and Europe have the same view on the need for UN reform and restructuring of the UNSC. Although the EU does not have a common position on UNSC reform, it has taken note of India's credentials to be a UNSC member. Most EU member-states support an expanded and restructured UNSC consisting of India and Japan.

The EU's desire for greater engagement with Asia is also driven by its concerns over growing regional uncertainties. The situation in

Afghanistan, developments in Iraq, the Middle East Peace Process and the continuing international debate on Iranian and North Korean nuclear ambitions make it inevitable for the EU to stay engaged with Asia and maintain a dialogue process with its strategic partners such as India, China and Japan as well as with regional groups.

We are already seeing concrete results of this engagement in the form of the agreement which the EU-3 (France, Britain and Germany) were able to broker with Iran on its nuclear program. A variation on this engagement is the dialogue of three civilizations—India-Russia-China. They represent nearly three billion of today's human population and the best of Europe and Asia.

The EU is also seriously concerned about the growing menace of terrorism. With increasing realization of terrorism's repercussions on Europe, the EU is serious about involving Asian states in the fight against terrorism. The EU recognizes now that all terrorism is interlinked, and open and democratic societies are particularly vulnerable since terrorists abuse the very freedom and liberty offered by these societies. The need for cooperation with regard to weapons of mass destruction, narcotics and cyber crime, besides terrorism, will lead to a strengthened dialogue between Asia and Europe.

Asia, with its diverse religions, ethnicities and cultures, has provided a model of syncretic evolution of civilization. India, with the second-largest Muslim community in the world, is a paradigm of Asia's syncretic culture and of how Islam can flourish in a plural, democratic and open society. The problems of religious extremism and fundamentalism also beset Europe with its expanding and increasingly diversified population. This is an area where Europe and India could exchange notes in order to benefit from their respective experiences.

The most persuasive argument for engagement between Europe and Asia is an economic one. In the evolving interdependent linkages, Asian nations are placed at a vantage point, which will make it inevitable for the EU to stay engaged. A large population of over three billion with significant consumer power will make Asia an attractive market for EU products.

In the areas of manufacturing and investment, the demographics will significantly change the way EU does its business with the world.

Here again, regions with significant young populations who have adequate skills will make them attractive locations for manufacturing, i.e., if we are to believe that market forces will determine the future. A graying Europe will seek to shift its manufacturing base to Asian countries, taking advantage of their skilled, reasonably-salaried manpower not only for products for local consumption but also for exports to third countries, including to the European markets themselves. This would entail greater cooperation between Asia and Europe in the WTO.

Science and technology provides yet another common ground for Europe and Asia. Both in fundamental and applied research, there will be greater synergies between the EU and Asian enterprises. India has already leapfrogged to the front ranks of nations engaged in cutting-edge technologies. Its skills in IT and biotechnology are world-renowned. China, Japan, South Korea and Southeast Asian countries will all become hubs for germinating new ideas and conceptualizing them.

All these are also interlinked to management of migration flows. Movement of natural persons in a seamless environment would become a logical fallout and therefore the challenge ahead for both the EU and Asia is how to manage migration flows.

Environment, sustainable development and energy are interlinked. While Asia will continue to depend on greater energy sources, including alternative sources such as renewable energy, it will also continue to depend a great deal on the technology of Europe for harnessing them. This dependence will inevitably forge a synergic relationship in energy. The EU's concern over environment is another factor which will bring it closer to a dialogue with Asia because, through sustainable development, it would seek to minimize the negative fallouts on climate change.

It therefore appears safe to say that as the 21st century enters its first decade, both Asia and Europe will come together as natural partners. The foundation for this partnership has already been laid through the varied dialogue processes: ARF, the EU Summit level interactions with India, China and Japan, APEC, ASEM, and the EU's intensified interaction with regional groupings including SAARC and OIC.

Now for a word on India's own ties with the European Union. These relations are broad-based and intensive. As Prime Minister Manmohan

Singh said, "India and EU are natural partners. Our relations are based on shared values of democracy, pluralism, rule of law, a free press and an independent judiciary. Our partnership has evolved over the years from economic and development cooperation to a broad-based engagement on a wide range of issues." Closer political consultations and a dynamic business relationship, underpinned by a shared commitment to democracy, are the main pillars of India's engagement with the EU.

THE ROLE OF GOVERNMENTS

What we need today is a new blueprint for development which will bring together the synergies of governments, the private sector, international organizations, scientists, the mass media and all civil society stakeholders, to end poverty-induced hunger. Each has a complementary contribution without which the battle cannot be won.

The role and responsibilities of governments are primary, whether these are at the national or international level. It is well-known that the OECD countries spend a billion dollars a day on agricultural subsidies to ensure their agricultural products are competitive in the international marketplace. Therefore, instead of providing greater access to products from agriculture-dependent developing countries and helping them muster the economic strength to fight hunger and poverty, the wealthiest countries of the world have set themselves up as competitors of the poorest.

At the same time, there is evidence of chronic aid fatigue, as seen in falling levels of development assistance, even as the world acknowledges that US$50 billion are required annually to meet the Millennium Development Goals, of which halving the numbers of the hungry is but one. The stark reality is that it is easier to fork out US$360 billion per year to make rich farmers richer than contribute US$50 billion to end poverty and hunger in the world.

As developed countries and international organizations repeat the mantra that good national governance is the panacea for all ills, what is apparent is the poverty of ethics in international governance.

The responsibility of national governments lies not only in ensuring that there is adequate production and availability of food to feed the people, but also, to ensure that the food reaches all. India has shown that this is possible by harnessing technology and adopting successful innovations such as the Green Revolution. We also have a national public distribution system, which is, I believe, the largest program of its kind in the world. Since independence, India has been able to increase its food production from about 55 million tons to over 200 million tons—an increase of over 250%, making the country completely self-sufficient and supporting its emergence as a net exporter. This has been made possible through huge public investments in irrigation, infrastructure, land reforms, increased use of fertilizers and research to introduce high-yielding crop varieties.

Comment

Anand G. Mahindra
Vice-Chairman and Managing Director, Mahindra & Mahindra Ltd.

In this essay, I pinpoint first the key developments in the global arena in the last few years and examine how, if at all, they would impact the four projected 'India scenarios.' Within the latter discussion, I will add my own observations on how these new events and situations might influence India's future alternatives and choices. Finally, I will attempt to summarize the incremental imperatives for India, if India were to have a shot at the ideal—though marginally modified—*Lion in the Emblem* scenario.

So what has changed in India of late? Obviously, a great deal, but I will enumerate only four changes that are of the greatest relevance to India's geopolitical strategy.

First, and most obviously, the invasion of Iraq that occurred in 2003 and the aftermath of the quick victory have been a mixed blessing for the United States. The consequences of the war and its impact on the Islamic world have important implications for India's future strategy.

Second, the peace initiative sparked off by Vajpayee, India's former prime minister, and robustly responded to by President Musharraf has also led to a number of new opportunities for the subcontinent.

Third, the Israeli-Palestinian conflict stubbornly refuses to move off center-stage, and the recent assassination, by Israeli forces, of the Hamas supreme leader, threaten to heighten polarization between Islamic nations and the western world on a scale hitherto unseen.

Fourth, India began 'shining', economically speaking, from the second half of 2003, and the emergence of a 'feel proud' factor, as opposed to a merely 'feel good' factor, has provided a momentum for reforms that was unanticipated just one year ago.

Add to this the fact that the Pakistani economy has been no laggard, and has been 'shining' as well, and you have a potential new dynamic for Indo-Pak relations.

What is the impact of all these developments on the India scenarios?

If you look at the *Frog in the Pond* scenario, it is evident that it was built on the premise that both India and Pakistan would remain mired in a stubbornly suspicious and belligerent attitude to each other, and would define their external affairs and strategies with principal reference to each other and to Kashmir. History, however, has often been dramatically altered by individual personalities, and in this case, both the former prime minister, Vajpayee, and President Musharraf have shown a new determination to lift their feet out of the quicksand.

Vajpayee had withstood opposition from constituents within his party and pressed ahead on his vision of reconciliation. His strategy of cricket diplomacy has proven successful, and clearly 'kismet' was on his side as the one-day match series resulted in neither side humiliating the other, thus leading to unprecedented scenes of camaraderie and bonhomie in the match venues. To make things even better for him, India won the final, and as scenes of victory and goodwill were beamed to an audience of over three-quarters of a billion people in the subcontinent, Vajpayee appeared to be a statesman of great prescience. This has strengthened his cards immeasurably in the task of pushing for reconciliation with Pakistan.

Accompanying these reconciliation initiatives will inevitably be opportunities for both countries to shape new objectives and roles for themselves on the international stage. President Musharraf has declared that he will eliminate Al Qaeda in Pakistan, and is positioning himself as a frontline fighter against terrorism and a visionary who could create a modern and moderate Islamic state that would be a template for others.

In order to sustain their new-found status in the world, both leaders will understand the importance of sustained economic progress, and since their economies have benefited immensely from liberalization and tariff reductions, it is unlikely that they will opt for circumspect economic policies with respect to the world or each other, as is envisaged in the *Frog in the Pond* scenario. Hence, I would posit that there has been a great reduction in the probability of this scenario.

The *Cobra in the Hole* scenario has not been given much credence thus far. It is even less credible today, given the developments since that time. India has been an activist of sorts in WTO forums, together with Brazil and South Africa, but has not taken any stance inimical to integration with the world economy. In fact, the target of its aggression has been agricultural subsidies and protectionism in the developed world, and its posture is no longer one of defending and delaying the opening-up of its own bastion.

Even in its diplomatic stance, India has been far from inward-looking. On the contrary, Vajpayee has probably logged more international air miles in the past 12 months than any prime minister in the past. I should know, having followed the former prime minister and Confederation of Indian Industry delegations practically all over the globe in an attempt to keep pace with him! In all these trips, both the political and industrial leadership of India adopted new, more self-assured approaches with the hosts, demanding and receiving a measure of respect as a potent economic force that had been dormant in the past. In summary, therefore, the *Cobra in the Hole* scenario deserves, once again, to be shelved.

For very similar reasons as those mentioned above, the *Calf in the Shadow* scenario should also be put aside for the moment. There is no doubt that Indo-U.S. relations have come a long way since the days of the Cold War, when India was perceived to be aligned with the Soviet bloc. The mutual suspicion that was pervasive in the days of Indira Gandhi and Nixon has been replaced by a perception of mutual objectives and interest, initially articulated during Clinton's regime. Economic liberalization has also brought, in its wake, as in so many other emerging nations, a widespread fascination and aspiration for the American lifestyle.

Yet, despite these growing bonds, Indians would never tolerate a government that adopted an openly servile and subordinate posture vis-à-vis the U.S. This is so not just because of some vestiges of historical suspicion, but also because Indians are individuals first, and fiercely proud of their cultural identity and independence. They are happy to assimilate and incorporate American culture into a unique Indian 'soup'. But they ultimately dance to their own subcontinental rhythms and are willing prisoners to their own Bollywood potboilers despite the welcome they have accorded MTV and Hollywood. They see their ties with the U.S growing day by day, as the Indian diaspora grows in size and influence in the U.S. They also know that their two democracies have no alternative but to strengthen their alliance. However, both the elite and the masses of

India want to see respect when they look into an American's eyes, and are willing to work hard on their economic status to earn it. The condescension with which most Indians view the relationship of Pakistan with the U.S is clear evidence that Indians will not accept being 'calves in the shadow'.

So that leaves us with the obviously ideal scenario of the *Lion in the Emblem*. Most people would without much doubt acknowledge that the signs today point towards the likelihood of India taking this path. Economically, the situation is clearly more encouraging than in the past, and at the close of the fiscal year on 31 March, 2004, more people rather than fewer had believed the growth rate would nudge the 8.5% mark.

Undoubtedly, a robust monsoon played a significant role, but the impressive growth rate was achieved despite very lukewarm industrial and manufacturing growth. In the last few months of the fiscal year, there was clear evidence that investment and industrial output were finally beginning to move up substantially, and this should act as a buffer in the next year against the effects of poor rainfall.

More important than anything else is perhaps the psychological mindset of the country's entrepreneurs and youth. They believe that India is finally at the proverbial 'lift-off' stage, and that Indian businesses have reached a level of maturity where they need not be overly concerned about coping with global competitors.

Such optimism should not be confused with euphoria and the onset of a bubble. Rather, it is the function of a long-overdue resurgence of self-esteem and self-confidence that was virtually destroyed during the many years of colonial rule. The physical and economic tangibles of colonialism are easily removed—the mental yoke is much harder to discard.

Had this phenomenon occurred overnight, it might have disappeared just as quickly. However, many factors have conspired over the past decade to bring about this mindset. Among these factors are the successful turnaround of Indian businesses and their achievements, domestically and globally; the incredible performance of the Indian IT sector and the powerful branding it has given to Indian brainware; and the coming of age of the Indian diaspora in business, politics and the arts, in the West. This attitudinal change provides hope that there will be momentum generated towards becoming the 'lions' of our emblem.

The scenario, when originally conceptualized, envisaged 'close relations with Europe, Russia, Iran and China'. In effect, Vajpayee's many forays abroad have indeed achieved this objective.

The principal difference in the international sphere versus the original scenario, however, is that Pakistan is not yet moving towards being a failed state, nor is there any evidence of secession by Sindh and Balochistan. On the contrary, Musharraf appears to still be in control, although very much a *Calf in the Shadow* of the U.S. In fact, Pakistan may just be following the script of the latter scenario!

The real opportunity for India is derived ironically from the deepening polarization between the Islamic world and the West. It is clear today that although the U.S. campaign in Iraq achieved the objective of ousting Saddam, the victory may yet be a Pyrrhic one. Al Qaeda is by no means an extinguished force, and even if Osama is located or eliminated, his martyrdom is almost a given. The Islamic world, joined by many other third world nations, has only been inflamed by what is perceived as the arbitrary deployment of America's hegemonic military might. Jihadis are only encouraged by disproportionately superior opponents—a sort of 'David and Goliath' syndrome—and not deterred by them.

The recent Israeli assassination of the Hamas leader is unfortunately not seen as completely distinct from U.S. actions. To an inflamed and vengeful mind, the two actions are part of one monolithic campaign to marginalize Islam.

In this volatile atmosphere, it is useful to remember that India is home to the second-largest population of Muslims in the world. If India can forge a détente with Pakistan, it will automatically give confidence and reassurance to the Muslims in India that they are unlikely to be viewed even by right-wing elements as a 'fifth column' within the country.

Clearly, we need to distance ourselves from the kind of emotions and factors that incited the riots in Gujarat. If we can sustain our rate of economic growth and make concerted attempts to include Muslims in that growing prosperity, we will strengthen our secular fabric.

Simultaneously, we should applaud and encourage the adoption of economic reforms in Pakistan and try to further enhance its growth rate by opening up trade between us. This would give a far greater percentage of their population a stake in peace and growth, and diminish the attraction of a fundamentalist existence.

Without belaboring this point much further, I conclude by saying that India's greatest opportunity in the next decade is in providing a template of a secular democracy, one that demonstrates how the second-largest Muslim population in the world can reject fundamentalist ideologues and participate in a modern, prosperous, market economy. The *Lion in the Emblem* would be toothless without such an achievement.

MANUFACTURING

Scenario

Tarun Das
Chief Mentor, Confederation of Indian Industry

In India, the manufacturing sector accounts for 70% of industry. Hence, it has a significant role to play in the overall growth process. Growth in the manufacturing sector has typically been low. This thus leads to low industrial growth. The importance of industrial growth for the development of the economy is a fact known to all. In most high-growth economies, the manufacturing sector plays an important role in the growth process. Thus, an analysis of growth in the manufacturing sector and the sector's role in the growth of the economy is important.

Given our three scenarios of growth rates, we may try to predict the situation in the manufacturing sector in these cases. In the first case, the overall GDP growth is pegged at 5.5%. The growth in the three broad sectors, i.e. industry, agriculture and services, is assumed to be 5.55%, 2.5% and 7% respectively. The share of industry in GDP is expected to remain at 25%. The size of the industry is expected to increase to $246 billion by 2015 from $130 billion in 2003 (constant U.S. prices).

In the second case, the overall GDP growth has been taken to be 6.5%. The growth in industry, agriculture and services is assumed to be 8%, 3% and 7.5% respectively. The share of industry in GDP is expected to increase to 30%. The size of the industry is expected to increase to $334 billion by 2015 at constant U.S. prices.

For the third case, the overall GDP growth has been taken to be 8%. The growth in industry, agriculture and services is assumed to be 11%, 3% and 9% respectively. The share of industry in GDP is expected to increase to 38% by 2015. The size of the industry is expected to increase to $477 billion by 2015 at constant U.S. prices.

This gives an outline of how the different sectors, specifically the industrial sector, should perform to achieve high economic growth. We also try to look at how some reforms would affect this growth process.

Rationalization of energy costs and regulatory issues will raise industrial growth by at least 1.5% per year. Making credit available at international interest rates will stimulate investment and raise industrial growth by at least 1% per year. Maintaining logistics infrastructure will boost industrial performance by at least 1.5% per year. Further, an introduction of a comprehensive VAT across center and states will reduce compliance costs, remove price distortions and make the industry more competitive. This can contribute an additional 1% to industrial growth in the medium to long term. Reforms to reduce regulatory hassles will help revive investment in the country, accelerate domestic investment and bring in more foreign direct investment (FDI). This can contribute an additional 0.5% to industrial growth.

These five areas of reform can generate an extra 5.5% growth, taking industrial growth rate to over 11% per annum. However, it is important to understand that all these issues should be addressed simultaneously.

Global competition is going to increase in the future. The domestic industry has successfully withstood the onslaught of such competition in the last 13 years, since 1991. Indian companies like Hero Cycles, Bajaj Auto, Reliance Industries and ONGC have achieved international standards and global outreach. Similarly, Indian companies like Sundaram Fasteners, which has won the Deming Award several times, have made their mark as international producers of quality products. Outward foreign direct investment from Indian companies like Ranbaxy has been on the rise in recent years. Large multinational corporations have also been relying on the manufacturing capabilities of Indian companies. Tata Motors, for example, makes cars for global automakers.

In a best-case scenario, India will be one of the world's manufacturing hubs, similar to the role China is playing right now. India is currently best-known for its IT-outsourcing services—led by companies like Infosys and Wipro. It could play a similar role in the manufacturing industry. India has a long tradition of craftsmanship and engineering. With the support of its leading technical universities and fresh engineering graduates every year, India's manufacturing sector will be a strong and sustainable one.

Comment

Manvinder S. Banga
Chairman, Hindustan Lever Ltd.

INTRODUCTION

There is no doubt in anyone's mind that India must aim for the targeted economic growth of 8% over the next few years. And this growth has to be led by the manufacturing sector—firstly, because it is a force multiplier for GDP growth, and secondly, because it will create employment. The potential for employment generation in this sector is immense and this will have a spiraling effect on the overall economy.

Industry contributes a little over 26% of the overall GDP, a sharp contrast to most high-growth economies. In China, for example, manufacturing contributes more than 50% to the GDP. Most high-growth economies have witnessed manufacturing growth of more than 10% in the recent past. In most Asian countries, the growth of manufacturing was fueled by exports. In contrast, India's export performance has suffered from a lack of competitiveness in the manufacturing sector. Even in the developed countries, manufacturing contributes a larger share to GDP. Over the last five years, India's industrial growth had hovered around 5%. The year 1995/96, when growth reached 13%, can easily be said to be the golden year for Indian industry.

Are there lessons to be learnt from our golden years? Is there something to learn from high-growth economies that have demonstrated success in manufacturing? What are the areas within manufacturing which need to be pushed to achieve higher growth? What are the bottlenecks hindering our progress in this sector?

It might be useful to see the manufacturing sector and its challenges in the backdrop of the overall economic situation. The Indian economy has witnessed growth of about 5%, which is higher than most world economies but clearly lower than its ambitions. Inflation has been well-contained within 5% for the past four years. India has been privileged with high levels of food grain reserves—over 48 million tons. Its forex position is the best ever with high reserves of over $80 billion and the rupee has strengthened against the dollar. At 24%, the savings rate is very decent and provides room for investment in infrastructure projects, which will have a multiplier effect on the economy. Overall, this puts India in a very healthy position to steamroll growth.

However, a few concerns remain and these need to be addressed. Industrial investment has slowed in the last three years and employment growth is also near zero in both the public and private sectors. The high fiscal deficit of around 6% is also an area of concern. The Indian economy still depends on agriculture, and monsoons have a critical impact (although much lower now than before). In the recent past, farm incomes had been impacted by soft prices and rising input costs, which in turn affected overall economic growth and specifically, impacted manufacturing demand.

While recent estimates suggest GDP growth of over 6%, this is based largely on the premise of good monsoons and agriculture growth. The manufacturing sector can play an equally vital role in economic growth. However, there are a few areas that need to be addressed urgently.

Exports and Outsourcing

India can emerge as a preferred sourcing base for manufactured goods. This opportunity offers dual benefits—it will spur growth in manufacturing and it will lead to higher exports which would lead to higher forex and increased employment in export services.

India has enormous potential in manufactured exports and the challenge is to obtain a large share of the global market for manufactured goods. Other countries like Korea, Mexico, Thailand and China have all done this in the past and leveraged the power of manufactured exports to drive economic growth and raise their per capita incomes. India, with roughly similar intrinsic strengths, is a poor comparison in both absolute and relative terms—its manufactured exports are less than a third of those of Mexico, Korea or China, in terms of sheer numbers. But India clearly also has some big advantages—a large knowledge base, skilled manpower and engineering capability, to name a few.

And yet, the potential for outsourcing manufacturing remains largely untapped in India. Given Indian engineering and design skills as well as lower costs, there is a big opportunity to increase sourcing of auto components for global companies. We have made a fairly good start with electric motors for GE, gearboxes for Toyota, and alto for Suzuki, but there remains large and untapped potential.

Similarly, apparel could be another window of opportunity. In the fast-moving consumer goods (FMCG) sector, the top 20 companies generate sales of over US$450 billion. As consumption is largely driven by developed economies, most of the manufacturing is still located in high-cost regions and this could be another major area for India to accelerate growth.

Building sourcing as a business will fundamentally strengthen the manufacturing sector, making it more cost-competitive and improve its overall quality. The global dimension would also often result in higher innovation in products and processes, all benefiting the domestic sector. It will also result in scale benefits, thus complimenting the domestic sector with cost reductions.

Quality and Image

Image is a critical area, and we cannot suffer from poor quality or image. The average quality levels in Indian manufacturing firms are perceived to be much lower than their competitors in the global arena. Also, the majority of India's exports are not from within high-tech areas. High-technology products are just 4% of total manufactured exports whereas for economies like China, Korea, Taiwan, Brazil. High-tech exports are 20-30% of manufactured exports. Developing high-tech manufacturing and exports is strongly inter-related with improving India's perceived image. India needs to drive its industry to be competitive and to be known for quality and reliability.

Another area that needs to be addressed is innovation and R&D. Over 70 multinationals including GE, Eli Lilly, Hewlett-Packard and Daimler-Chrysler have set up R&D facilities in India in the last five years. However, R&D expenditure as a proportion of GDP continues to be very low. There is an urgent need to address the area of innovation and R&D. There is a need to step up commitment to indigenous innovation and development. Greater collaboration amongst the troika of government-industry-academia can lend impetus to this area. Innovation is vital for image leadership as well as the stimulation of demand. India must capitalize on its large skills base and ensure it drives higher rates of innovation, improvements in quality and image leadership. This will also open up avenues in high-tech manufacturing and design, an area which is largely dominated by developed countries.

Customer service is also an important determinant of image and competitiveness. India must build a world-class service mindset and equally, implement processes to deliver this. The country must leverage its skills in IT to improve connectivity and integrate supply chains. A robust supply chain is the backbone of good manufacturing.

Costs

Labor costs in India are low and this is an advantage. However, India's advantage in low labor costs is negated by low productivity.

Overall productivity is low largely because the majority of the labor force is in the unorganized sector—small-scale industries (SSIs) where value addition is low. Productivity is also impacted by the relatively lower scale of operations. Reservations and tax exemptions to SSIs are big deterrents for expansion. This means that India is not able to fully exploit economies of scale or improve process efficiencies. A case in point is the textile industry.

Apart from pruning the list of industries in the SSI sector, the government can lead the initiative in aggregating SSI units, in order to obtain better bargaining power in sourcing raw materials as well as marketing products. Doing this will enable them to take the technology leap as well as overcome issues of economies of scale. Technology modernization is a challenge to be tackled across industries in order to drive productivity. India needs to develop different models for harnessing the collective power of these fragmented units to stimulate industrial growth.

Another key issue is the cost of power. This is an issue both when you consider from the tariff perspective as well as in terms of the reliability of supply. Erratic power supply leads to more shutdowns and therefore higher costs of manufactured goods. The financial health of the State

Electricity Boards (SEBs) is also an area of concern. The privatization of distribution is a move in the right direction as evidenced in the case of Delhi. It is critical that power sector reforms are undertaken speedily to ensure better, reliable and cheaper power.

We must drive industry productivity and process excellence, and achieve the standards set by the Japanese Institute of Plant Maintenance (JIPM) in its award, Total Productive Maintenance (TPM).

Productivity of capital, labor and all resources must be a paramount objective when addressing costs.

Infrastructure

Infrastructure is a key issue which still needs to be addressed. Infrastructure is a long-term investment. In economic terms, the objective is not to optimize in the short run but to benefit in the long term. India's overall infrastructure—roads, power, ports etc.,—needs to be improved considerably as it impacts costs as well as supply chain efficiency and service.

Multi-modal optimality should be explored in the area of transportation. This represents potential opportunity, given India's large water resources and railway network. Increasing the involvement of the private sector is one measure which can hasten changes in infrastructure. BOT ('build-operate-transfer') projects, in increasing efficiency in execution and operation, have made enormous improvements to urban transport and port infrastructure. The National Highway Development Project (NHDP), which includes improvements in road connectivity to the major ports, and the 'Golden Quadrilateral' Project which connects the four metros, are landmark projects both in terms of scale and structuring.

Fiscal Rationalization

The existing tax structure in the country is complex and tax levels are high. Each state has a different sales tax structure, with varying rates and exemptions. Higher tax rates increase the cost of products and thereby lower consumer demand. They also lead to higher transaction costs in the economy. The taxation structure needs to be simplified to ease tax administration and widen the tax net. Levies are to be rationalized and measures adopted to develop a friendlier and more practical fiscal regime. The tax rates should be comparable to those in the developing countries. Apart from the above benefits, it will bring down the cost of doing business in India. Nationwide implementation of VAT is a right step in this direction.

Regulatory and Investment Climate

India continues to suffer from poor process efficiency both in industry and government. Multiple touchpoints and clearances lead to inordinate delays in project implementation. This is best reflected in the fact that in the last decade, only 50% of approved FDI translated into actual inflows.

As a result, the FDI inflow into India is less than a tenth of that in China. FDI as a percentage of GDP is just 0.5% for India compared to 4.1% for China. FDI inflows have in fact stagnated in the last four years when they should have been growing aggressively.

Increasing FDI will directly enable India to step up investments in the economy. FDI will also encourage marketing investments, thus fueling demand. Transfer of global innovation will be much speedier, again improving demand. FDI can also facilitate growth of sourcing in the area of manufactured exports. Complexity and delay in regulatory processes must be substantially reduced in order to attract higher levels of FDI inflows.

A simplified regulatory framework and a positive investment climate are critical in attracting investments in the manufacturing sector. A modified regulatory framework would include a reduction in the number of permissions and approvals required. The regulator should be totally independent from the government or any other stakeholder. Regulation should be consistent. There is also a need to prevent a tangle of bureaucracy which happened in the telecommunications sector where multiple regulators emerged over time.

Labor reforms are equally critical. Labor laws need to be amended to become more relevant in the current context. Privatization and divestments are integral to reforms and for creating the right sentiment of change.

CONCLUSION

There is a need to step up the pace of change. To attract FDI, India will need to address many of the above issues. The pace will critically determine a shift from caution to optimism among global players.

In conclusion, it can only be said that India must engage fervently in its attempts to step up growth in manufacturing. The reform process must be hastened and an enabling climate created. Equally, India must address infrastructure and operational efficiencies.

The manufacturing sector can indeed take the lead and drive economic growth. Technological modernization, industrial reforms and infrastructural investments are the right enablers. There are valuable lessons to be learnt from other countries in some fields; in many others, India needs to innovate. The real test is in the speed and quality of execution of this roadmap.

India's objective should be to move up to the next stage of value creation and to enhance its presence in high technology exports, design and R&D. India must target manufacturing growth of more than 10% and achieve our goal of 8% GDP growth.

Comment

Sunil Kant Munjal
Managing Director, Hero Corporate Services

India is far more linked to the global economy today than ever before. There has been much talk about whether India will achieve 8% GDP growth and the necessary drivers required to help India achieve this growth. In August 2002, the World Economic Forum and the Confederation of Indian Industry, at the India Economic Summit, presented several scenarios on desirable improvements in physical as well as financial infrastructure with different assumptions on the rate of GDP growth.

One of the scenarios dealt with manufacturing and it was unequivocally stated that for India to sustain an 8% overall growth, this industry had to grow at 11%. Since manufacturing constitutes 70% of the Indian industry, a high growth in this sector is clearly essential for 11% industrial growth.

While work needs to be done in various areas, such as in the areas of exports, capital and labor productivity, infrastructure, fiscal rationalization, quality and image of products, regulatory and investment climate and labor reforms, to accelerate industrial growth, this paper focuses on a few key factors on the front-end and back-end of the business.

As these factors are internal to the industry, the industry needs to initiate measures on these factors to give them a greater push. These factors are namely, improving the effectiveness and productivity of all the resources, including labor, capital and technology, to compete globally; expanding market reach through a higher thrust on exports; and, constant innovation to meet the market needs at competitive costs. These factors also highlight the need for a skilled manpower base and building a 'unique selling point' (USP) as sub-factors. Labor market reforms and increasing exports through policy measures will also require some support from the government.

Let us observe the evolution of the Indian manufacturing sector over the last few decades. During the decades of the fifties to the eighties, the Indian markets were protected by high import barriers. Import duties had even gone up to a peak rate exceeding 800%. The GDP CAGR growth in the same period went from 3.2% in the 1950s to 5.7% in the 1980s.

After the introduction of economic reforms in India in 1991, markets opened up and liberalization brought with it many changes. GDP growth touched a peak of 7.5% annually in the period 1994-97 though it averaged nearly 5% a year subsequently. Import duties came down to 30%. Reduction in import duties meant that the prices of Indian products were much more aligned to global prices, compared to two decades earlier. In an economy protected by high tariffs, manufacturers could pass on the costs of inefficiency and low productivity by way of higher value of goods produced. When these values are compared internationally, they are far below those claimed by the local manufacturer. As a result, the economy could post GDP growth, part of which was 'illusory'. Compare this with an economy which has the same GDP (in absolute terms) but which prices its goods more closely to their global prices. GDP growth in the latter economy could rightfully be termed as 'real', as opposed to 'illusory' in the former.

Today, India is far more efficient and productive, as it prices its goods and services at near global parity (as peak import duties have come down) when compared to the era of the 1980s and consequently, the GDP growth rate in India is currently 'real', not 'illusory'.

In December 2003, the mood of the Indian economy was extremely positive. The Indian rupee had strengthened from INR49 to US$1, to INR45.55 to US$1, forex reserves had crossed US$100 billion, the stock markets were booming and corporate results had been better than they had been in the last seven years. Goldman Sachs (a global investment bank) had predicted that India would become the world's third-largest economy, after China and USA, by 2050 A.D., dwarfing Japan and Germany. Of the current G6 economies (U.S., Japan, Germany, France, Italy and UK), only the U.S. and Japan may be among the six largest economies in U.S. dollar terms in 2050. Brazil and Russia will be the other two economies in the top six by 2050.

Having said this, in order for India to be globally competitive, it has to tackle the issue of increasing productivity more seriously. In today's competitive environment, particularly under the World Trade Organization (WTO) imperatives, the importance of productivity is not limited to capital and labor productivity.

Productivity now also has to include the contributions of technology and managerial decisions in sustaining a high rate of output growth. This means that the effect of technological progress, higher asset velocity, improved skills of labor including multi-tasking, on-the-job training, and adoption of best management practices, corporate culture and work ethics are all important factors that determine overall productivity improvements.

Achieving sustained growth calls for higher productivity. Timely techno-managerial strategies therefore become imperative. While some industries require simple remedies like substituting wheel-barrows for loads carried atop construction workers' heads, other industries will require product, land and labor market reforms.

With major improvements in transportation, logistics and information technology, localized manufacturing has given way to cross-border multi-staged production processes. In such a scenario, where the value chain has been sliced, more countries are included in the production network and therefore, countries need to be aware of their relative cost-competitiveness in the short run as well as ensure quality output, so as to remain important cogs in the larger regional and global production system.

Outsourcing of manufacturing products from India got a boost in the year 2003 with the Japanese Institute of Plant Maintenance (JIPM) awarding Total Productive Maintenance (TPM) awards to 18 Indian plants from 10 firms. This was the first time 10 Indian firms were recognized in one year for achieving world-class productivity levels.

At the front-end, businesses need to expand their market reach by focusing on exports. Market reach would be possible if India becomes the preferred sourcing base for manufactured goods. Indian exports will further get a boost due to the signed trade agreement with Thailand. India is also working on another agreement with Singapore.

Foreign Direct Investment (FDI) can be a powerful tool for export growth. There are a number of reasons why the role of FDI in promoting exports from India is poor, and efforts need to be made by the government to remove obstacles to FDI in India.

Export performance can be improved by the lowering of import tariffs. Lowering import tariffs benefits exports as the costs of inputs would be lower. Increase in imports would also cause the dollar demand to increase and create market pressure to depreciate the rupee which would in turn, again, help exports.

In case it is perceived that the exchequer shall forego indirect tax collections, it can be argued that both the above factors will also serve to increase the rupee value of imports, which is the tax base, and thus offset, to some extent, the impact of tariff cuts on gross tax collected by the government.

Exports will also be aided if the Indian industry carves out distinctly a 'unique selling point' (USP) for itself. Currently, the principal USP, both in domestic and global markets, is price. This is an advantage India has enjoyed as a result of the last decade of reforms and Indian corporations have really worked hard to straighten the glitches in the supply chains—distribution and delivery systems are far leaner than ever before. But cutting costs and improving efficiency can get a company to compete only on price, in order to sustain margins and profitability. As it was in the services segment for example, telecommunications service providers and housing loan companies battle on price and interest rates, respectively. Such situations make competitors indistinguishable from one another.

India Inc. therefore, needs to develop a unique strength which will increase its salience both in the global and domestic markets, and this can come about through excellence in innovation. Indian industry can use innovation to define its competitive advantage for the same reason that makes it an attractive base for low-cost, quality operations—its large scientific manpower base. The challenge is that innovation is never an easy sell because it cannot promise a quick return, and because there is always the proverbial challenge of changing organizational mindset and culture to overcome.

Summing up, higher growth in the manufacturing sector is needed for an economy like India as it works towards creating jobs and demand for products. The industry must work actively to widen the base of skilled manpower and knowledge workers as well as increase productivity, to enable its products to be priced competitively around the globe. Every company should work to create unique differentiators that allow them to compete not only on price and quality, but on other factors too, including innovation in product manufacturing and service delivery.

If the industry wants a vibrant manufacturing sector, action has to begin at home. It is indeed heartening to note that a good start has been made—Indian manufacturing is coming of age both in the domestic and world markets. The country is on the threshold of good economic growth, propelled by the services and manufacturing sectors. India is also entering a take-off stage with the economy having reached a critical mass—it can now launch itself into a high growth orbit and take its rightful place in the developed world by the turn of this decade.

A good beginning has already been made in this direction in the auto component industry. Today, almost all global auto OEMs have their international purchasing offices in India and all of them are very bullish on sourcing from India. Success stories abound in the Indian auto component industry—Bharat Forge, Sundaram Fasteners, Rico Auto, Hitech Gears, to name a few.

Indian companies are fast becoming Tier 1 and Tier 2 companies to all the global auto majors. And the manufacturing success story is not only confined to the auto industry. Garments have long been India's flag bearer for manufactured goods exports. It is further heartening to note that the Indian industry has become leaner and more cost-efficient as it competes in the world markets. The last three years have seen Indian manufacturing costs trimmed across the industry sectors and also across all cost goods—be it lower investments, better supply chain management, swapping high interest loans with softer loans, or radical quality improvements. Today, the Indian manufacturing industry is increasingly competitive in terms of cost, and this, along with world-class quality, gives a promising picture of the future.

TRADE AND FOREIGN INVESTMENT

Scenario

Tarun Das
Chief Mentor, Confederation of Indian Industry

Trade plays an important role in the growth of the economy. After the opening up of the economy, its role has become even more significant for India. Its performance, though, has fluctuated throughout the decade. Even though the external sector has grown in India, foreign trade to GDP ratio is low compared to similar growing economies.

Another area of concern is that India's terms of trade are deteriorating. Imports are becoming costlier than exports. In addition, although the nominal exchange rate has declined, the real exchange rate has appreciated. This has further made exports uncompetitive. Even though foreign investment has increased during the last decade, yet as a proportion of GDP, it is still lower than other developing countries like China.

With this background, we try to look at our three scenarios. For a growth of 5.5%, import to GDP ratio should be pegged at 10.8% and export to GDP ratio at 7.6%. Without any major incentive to boost investor confidence, foreign investment may decline marginally and hover around the savings-investment gap. With an overall growth rate of 6.5%, import to GDP ratio should be pegged at 12% and export to GDP ratio at 7.6%. Foreign investment would increase from 1.3% of GDP to 1.9%. In the third case, with an overall growth rate of 8%, import to GDP ratio should be pegged at 13%. Foreign investment would increase to 2.75% of GDP. The expected changes in exports, trade deficit and foreign investment in the three cases are given in the following table.

	2002-03	**2015**		
		5.5% growth	6.5% growth	8% growth
Exports	49	92	120	157
Trade deficit	8.1	16.4	13.1	7.3
Foreign investment	6.6	6	21	34.7

(All figures are in $ billion and projections are at constant prices.)

Next, we take a look at the reforms that are required, and how they would affect the growth rates. Reducing the number of clearances and improving efficiency of government machinery at both central and state levels can increase inflows by at least 50%. Quicker decision-making on privatization would also attract higher FDI inflow. Also, in infrastructure development, removing restrictions and implementing measures for boosting investor confidence would contribute to increases in FDI inflow. This, in turn, would be important for the growth of the economy.

From the outset, India's predominant economic thinking has been very much linked to defending, protecting and safeguarding the country's interests. This translates into, for instance, restricting foreign labor and barring external investments in certain sectors such as retail.

Since the start of the reforms, however, foreign investment has been increasingly welcome, but only in priority areas. It has not been encouraged in those areas where the foreign investor is perceived as coming into the market for his own profit-making objectives. The Indian model of economic development is certainly at a crossroads, oscillating between the open and restricted market as well as between collectivist guidance and pure individualism.

To identify the specific characteristics of a potential Indian model of economic development, it is important to review other established models applied in today's world. These are namely, the so-called Western or Anglo-Saxon model, and the East Asian model which developed in Japan, Korea, China and other parts of East Asia.

THE WESTERN MODEL: INDIVIDUALISM—OPEN MARKETS

The so-called Western model began to take shape from the late 1970s, mainly in the U.S. and the UK, after decades in which a more interventionist model had been in use. In general, there was a transfer away from the state to the private domain. In this model, the state enters the market not as a player. It neither owns businesses nor invests in them. Its role is solely to maintain overall competitiveness.

Anglo-Saxon economies have favored the system of a more 'residual' welfare state, with reduced tax rates and flexible labor markets where there are many incentives for seeking employment. The state plays the role of compensator of last resort rather than that of a universal provider of welfare and social benefits. The model largely relies on the market co-ordination of economic agents and seeks to address market failures by providing additional market elements wherever they are missing.

The model further demands the presence of well-functioning and transparent markets to allocate resources freely and efficiently. Individuals make the majority of decisions on economic activities and transactions but the market is the venue in which these transactions are executed. As a result, the market becomes an important medium for governing the terms of transactions.

The model of unfettered free markets may work well in developed markets like North America and parts of Europe. The Anglo-Saxon model of well-functioning markets that allocate resources efficiently was demonstrably a failure when applied to developing markets. As the recent history of Argentina shows, immediate liberalization and total market opening may lead to the destruction of the socio-economic base of a developing country[1]. However, the model may be well-suited for ripe economies like the UK in the 1980s when Margaret Thatcher introduced sweeping reforms.

The Anglo-Saxon model is not the only approach adopted by Western industrialized nations. Despite global economic integration and considerable harmonization of the financial markets, the distinctive characteristics

1 Japan's rapid industrialization after WWII was possible because the state guided and directed the economy. Behind the state was what is often referred to as the 'iron triangle' of elites—ministry officials, politicians and executives of the big conglomerates. The spirirt of this Japanese model comes across in the epithet 'Japan Inc'. As this label suggests, Japan had managed to develop a collective cohesion via which the country succceeded in creating economic success. This model was later applied elsewhere in East Asia, particularly in President Park Chung-hee's South Korea, Prime Minister Mahathir Mohamad's Malaysia and Prime Minister Lee Kuan Yew's Singapore. See Richter, F J (2000). *The East Asian Economic Development Model: Economic Growth, Institutional Failure and the Aftermath of the Crisis*. London: Macmillan.

and economic functions of national economic systems have not necessarily been undermined.

In continental Europe, particularly in Germany and France, government intervention has been widely accepted. The model has been called the 'social market economy', because markets have not been left totally to the free interaction of the market powers. In Germany, for instance, the welfare system which is financed by contributions and backed by the state, provides security for the individual, and has persisted despite powerful pressure for change. However, these pressures have taken their toll in recent years, moving European economies closer to the Anglo-Saxon model.

THE EAST ASIAN MODEL: COLLECTIVISM—RESTRICTED MARKETS

The governments of East Asian economies, first the Japanese then the Korean, Southeast Asian and finally the Chinese , adopted what is commonly referred to as an inward-oriented strategy of economic development. This model promotes industrialization by fostering industries to replace imports and stimulate production for the home market. A spurt of industrial growth ensued as many new industries were created, largely to produce simple consumer products and—after a further period of growth—technologically-sophisticated products. At a later stage, Asian governments adopted an outward-oriented strategy and pushed their domestic industries to export their products. This growth process, however, was diluted by the Asian Economic Crisis in 1997/98 when these governments pursued economic growth relentlessly, and many Asian firms targeted increased turnover instead of increased profits.

A key distinguishing feature of the East Asian model compared with its Western counterpart is that governments play an active role in the development process. This feature is based on the socio-economic fundamentals of Asian societies where collectivism—i.e. the betterment of the nation as a whole—is more important than individual increases in wealth. The Confucianist industrial culture in the East Asian countries—namely Japan, South Korea, China and parts of Southeast Asia—is based on the principle that cooperation amongst individuals is more important than self-seeking achievements. The development plans of these countries were remarkable because of the national policies adopted, with particular focus on growth with equity, clear strategies and a commitment to achieving it. This contrasts with the case in the Western world, particularly in the U.S. and the UK, where individuals rather than the government, make the majority of decisions. Other features of the East Asian model include high insider shares and weak roles for outsiders in corporate governance, close bank-firm relations and limited reliance on stock markets in investment financing, and relatively static labor markets.

Since the Asian Economic Crisis of 1997/98, there have been considerable adaptations to the original model. The thinking that guided the economic development of the East Asian nations has shifted from the previous over-emphasis on GDP to a more balanced people-oriented ideology. In addition, elements of the Western model have been incorporated, i.e. better corporate governance, more flexible labor markets and very pro-active calls for foreign direct investment. The last is particularly true in the case of China. However, the use of national policies and strong government guidance are still prevalent.

THE INDIAN MODEL: INDIVIDUALISM—RESTRICTED MARKETS

The economic thought of the former government was based largely on the concerns of the small businessmen who form the key constituency of the party. The former government has taken a relative laissez-faire approach to business and has been generally relaxed about the acquisition of wealth. This is in considerable contrast to the Nehruvian aversion to business and Gandhian asceticism.

The new Indian development model has moved considerably towards the Anglo-Saxon model on the one hand (positive attitudes towards the creation of wealth) and the East Asian model on the other hand (pro-active government policies to foster growth). Prime Minister Manmohan Singh appears to continue the economic reform process heralded by his predecessor. Nonetheless, the Indian economic model still displays particularities that distinguish it from the other two models.

Generally, markets are still restricted when it comes to the influx of consumer goods. The government embraces protectionist trade and investment policies. Under the swadeshi doctrine, the BJP has advocated restrictions on foreign investment with a view to protecting Indian business interests against those of multinational firms. This stands in stark contrast to the East Asian and the Chinese models of actively inviting foreign direct investment. Comparing India and China, the latter has an outward-looking development model where benefits are spread inward, towards home markets. In addition, China follows a manufacturing-based development model whereas India's model is service-based. On the other hand, India has a homegrown model of economic development which is now gaining global reach. Further, India has a well-developed banking system, vibrant capital markets, and most importantly, indigenous multinational companies and outstanding entrepreneurs. Each of these two nations has a distinctly different recipe for economic development—recipes that are complements rather than substitutes as they fit into the broad mosaic of globalization. However, India's main advantage over China is that economic growth is already based on a political system where the free play of power leads to the best allocation of resources.

The 'new Indian model' does certainly have its merits. It is based on the creative entrepreneurship of the individual—potentially inspiring an Anglo-Saxon driven wave of rapid economic growth. The model may also lead to longer-term sustainable benefits. India's homegrown entrepreneurs may give it a long-term advantage over China.This new Indian model is not a fixed dogma—it is a continuum moved mainly by reform initiatives from the Indian government. It is understood that the doctrine of swadeshi cannot be maintained forever. Current reform endeavors by Manmohan Singh's Congress-led government are leading to more active calls for foreign direct investment. The question of how successful the new Indian economic model will be in the future, and how it will emerge after further testing against the Western and the East Asian models, is best left to the future. The outcome, like most social and economic outcomes, is inherently unpredictable. Differing historical traditions will almost always intervene to make economic development unique to each nation. General—or even universal—theories meant to explain similar economic processes across cultures are almost certain to mislead.

Comment

Robert E. Kennedy
Harvard University

India is a country of vast resources, but it remains very poor. Why is this? In this book, different authors explore the potential and steps necessary to achieve 8% annual economic growth in the coming decade. The consensus among contributors is that India has the potential to increase its rate of growth, but it would require focused and potentially unpopular initiatives in five areas to achieve this.

1) Micro-economic liberalization and continued macro-economic stabilization. Key items include reforming land markets, eliminating most price regulations, liberalizing labor markets, controlling the fiscal deficit, reducing interest rates and improving infrastructure.
2) Energy sector reform. Key reforms include the separation of generation, transmission and distribution, reforming price regulation, privatization, and attracting foreign capital.
3) Financial sector reform. Key reforms include privatization, new legislation governing bankruptcy and foreclosure, developing the debt market, achieving capital account convertibility and attracting FDI.
4) Improved competitiveness in the manufacturing sector. Key items include changes to the existing labor laws, relaxing or eliminating small-scale reservations, reforming the VAT and investing in infrastructure.
5) Trade and investment reforms. Key reforms include simplifying and lowering tariffs, upgrading trade facilities (ports, airports, customs clearance facilities), dramatically simplifying FDI approval procedures and opening new areas to foreign investment.

India's development can only be achieved by embracing globalization. If the liberalization of trade and foreign investment is half-hearted, or if the country attempts to guide development with a heavy hand, India will remain poor and fall further behind its more outward-looking neighbors.

TRADE AND INVESTMENT AS A DEVELOPMENT DRIVER

History has shown that embracing the global economy is integral to economic development. Scan, for instance, the list of the world's most successful developing countries over the past 25 years—China, Chile, Egypt, Mexico, the Philippines, Poland and South Korea. Encouraging trade and foreign investment has been a central element of the successful reform programs in each of these countries in transition. At the other extreme, countries that have resisted globalization have generally lagged behind their more open neighbours—for example, Myanmar, the Ukraine, Venezuela, Zimbabwe…and India.

Engagement in international trade and investment is integral to development because it increases the productivity of local resources, which invariably leads to higher wages and better living standards. Free trade encourages a country to focus on those things it does relatively well, and to stop doing things it does relatively poorly (economists refer to this as comparative advantage). Most developing countries have many workers, but are relatively deficient in capital, infrastructure and the capacity to produce sophisticated products. Developing countries are thus better-off when they import capital and sophisticated products (e.g. airplanes, telecommunications equipment), and pay for them with exports of labor-intensive goods and services. Trade thus causes a shift from activities in which a country is comparatively less efficient to those in which it is comparatively more efficient.

Trade has a second important benefit. It increases the range and quality of options available to local consumers and forces local producers to improve their offerings in order to compete. Countries that have lowered their tariff barriers and increased the intensity of competition in the local market have often seen rapid improvements in productivity, as local producers rush to upgrade their products and processes.

There are two common misconceptions about globalization and development that deserve brief mention. First, many casual observers use a country's trade (or current account) balance as a measure of development success. The implicit assumption is that trade surpluses (exports) are good, while deficits (imports) are bad. But the purpose of trade is not to accumulate financial reserves, it is to facilitate the deployment of a country's productive resources in their highest value activities. Many rapidly developing countries have run persistent current account deficits which are funded by foreign capital inflows. Examples include Brazil in the 1960s and 1970s, Mexico under the North American Free Trade Agreement (NAFTA), Poland in the early 1990s and Portugal after it joined the EU. Trade policy is best assessed by how it affects domestic productivity, not whether it generates current account surpluses or deficits.

A second misconception is that developing countries should target sectors that pay high wages—such as aerospace, steel or high-tech manufacturing. But the reason these sectors have high wages is that they employ large amounts of capital per worker. Because capital is generally in short supply in developing countries, targeting capital-intensive (high wage) sectors is a recipe for failure. Living standards can only grow when a country employs all its factors of production efficiently.

Foreign direct investment (FDI) also leads to an array of benefits. In addition to providing capital that funds investment, foreign investors typically provide technology, links to supply and distribution chains, and management expertise. These factors raise the productivity of local resources, thus raising wages and the standard of living. Nearly all academic studies indicate that recipient countries realize many and varied benefits from foreign direct investment.

HOW DOES INDIA COMPARE?

Among major developing countries, India ranks very low on most measures of globalization. Three common measures are the trade-to-GDP ratio, the FDI-to-GDP ratio, and per capita FDI. Other developing countries are significantly more exposed to international trade and capital flows than is India, and each is much wealthier. For instance, China and Egypt have the least trade exposure—but both are still about 70% higher than India. Other large countries also receive significantly more inbound FDI than does India. Measured as a percentage of GDP, these countries average more than six times India's FDI inflows. Measured on a per person basis, the multiple is nearly 40. Imagine how Indian living standards would increase if annual FDI inflows rose from only US$2.24 to US$90 per person.

Many factors other than trade influence a country's standard of living. These include history, natural endowments and proximity to developed country markets. But experience and numerous academic studies indicate that openness to international trade and investment flows are critical ingredients for development. Raising political and procedural objections cannot erase the unpleasant fact that, among large developing countries, India ranks near the bottom on measures of global openness, and on income per person. Reluctance to embrace the global economy is not the whole story, but it is an important element of it.

OBSERVATIONS AND RECOMMENDATIONS

The purpose of trade and foreign investment is to increase domestic productivity, not to accumulate trade surpluses or foreign exchange reserves. Globalization is important because it allows domestic resources (labor, capital, land) to be put to their most efficient uses. This is accomplished in two ways. First, resources are shifted from low productivity sectors to higher productivity sectors. In most countries, agriculture has relatively low productivity per worker, manufacturing somewhat higher, and services even higher. A second mechanism is to raise output per worker in existing activities. Competition from foreign firms (via trade) and FDI both play key roles in raising the productivity of local producers.

The composition of global trade flows is shifting from manufactured goods towards trade in services. Since 1990, global trade in manufactured goods has grown at a 5.6% annual rate. Trade in services has grown at nearly 10%, with much faster growth in services exports from developing countries. India is well-positioned to lead and benefit from the shift towards trade in services. The country has a huge pool of English speakers, excellent technical education, traditional linkages to both European and North American markets, and an early headstart in both software and IT-enabled services. These sectors are projected to grow from about 1.4% to 7% of GDP over the next eight years, and account for more than 35% of India's export earnings by 2010. Government policy will be key. To date, the central government has pursued a policy of benign neglect. As the sector grows, the temptation to 'guide' its development will be strong. Government policy in the sector should focus on enabling legislation (such as telecommunications deregulation and efforts to promote entrepreneurship), not on industrial targeting or subsidies for favored sectors.

Regional trade opportunities should not be ignored. Economic linkages with ASEAN countries (Singapore, in particular) and with China should be deepened. Measured globally, the overwhelming majority of trade and investment flows occur within regions. There are potential gains from trade between India and Singapore—with India providing high-quality manpower and Singapore providing capital, links to international networks and management. India could serve as the back office to Singapore's head office, to the mutual benefit of both. Cross-border trade between China and Singapore is growing at double-digit rates. China and India are complements more than rivals—with China's strength in manufacturing complemented by India's potential in services.

Liberalization and deregulation will make investment more attractive to foreign firms. FDI increases domestic productivity. Higher productivity raises wages while keeping quality-adjusted prices low. These factors benefit consumers, raise local living standards and increase competitiveness. Increased competitiveness leads to rising exports and a flow of resources to the newly competitive sectors. This leads to new pressures for liberalization, and the virtuous cycle starts again. The entire cycle raises living standards for those in affected sectors. When the cycle works, it gradually encompasses more and more sectors, driving development across the economy.

Liberalization of trade and investment is vital, but also controversial. Globalization encounters fierce resistance from both government policymakers and local producers. Most policymakers (in every country) have a fundamental distrust of market forces and believe they can outwit the market, favoring some sectors and disadvantaging others. But history shows that this game is rarely successful.

The overwhelming share of experiments with industrial targeting (from Albania to Zimbabwe) have failed miserably. The success stories most often cited (Japan, Korea and Singapore) owe more to market forces than is commonly understood. Less virtuous policymakers are also drawn to trade and investment restrictions because they increase bureaucrats' power over the business sector and provide opportunities for corruption. Local producers benefit from protection as well. Most would prefer not to compete with tough, well-funded rivals from abroad. What better way to ensure high prices and orderly competition than to disadvantage potential foreign rivals? There are many sophisticated justifications for continued protection. These generally involve terms such as 'infant industry', 'strategic trade' and 'creating advantage'. Again, experience shows that the infants rarely grow up, nearly all sectors eventually are defined as 'strategic' and the projected advantages never materialize. Bureaucrats and industrialists can easily live with this state of affairs, but everyone else suffers.

The government must make a visible commitment to embrace the global economy. Because globalization will be disruptive, a phased approach may be appropriate. One widely popular option would be to commit to unifying tariff rates and lowering the top rate to 10% over a five-year period. This approach has jumpstarted growth in Chile, Poland and Mexico.

India should reform its investment laws so that the presumption is in favor of trade and investment, not against. A key component of this goal will be to streamline the approval process for foreign investment. Currently, potential investors in sectors such as power and mining must secure as many as 100 separate permits and clearances. Each causes delays, increases costs and provides the opportunity for corruption. Faced with such daunting obstacles, most foreign investors simply give up and invest elsewhere. The foreign investors lose a little, but India loses a lot. A single, central government investment office should be formed and granted the power to approve foreign investment. The states' ability to hold up foreign investors must be curtailed.

It is necessary to accelerate the privatization process and encourage foreign investors to participate. Moving public firms to the private sector exposes firms to competitive pressures and forces them to upgrade. In other markets, many privatized firms partner foreign firms to facilitate industrial upgrading. In fact, more than 75% of global FDI flows are M&A-related. India's slow pace of privatization holds back domestic productivity and is an impediment to FDI inflows.

It is also important to implement legislation to encourage foreign investment in infrastructure—including roads, ports, airports, energy and telecommunications. Foreign firms are more than willing to provide the capital for infrastructure improvement, if they are confident of realizing a return on their investments. International investors have played a major role in infrastructure sectors in Mexico, the Philippines and Egypt, with rapid results. The central government should eliminate investment restrictions, and loosen pricing restrictions in these sectors. It would also be very useful to make a blanket commitment to international arbitration of investment disputes.

With the exception of military-related sectors, all restrictions on foreign investment should be eliminated. FDI should be allowed in telecommunications, retail and wholesale distribution, the media, banking and insurance.

CONCLUSION

The country has tremendous human and economic resources, and has little to fear from globalization. The country must, however, overcome its historical reluctance to allow its citizens to freely engage with the outside world. Too often, policymakers have approached globalization as a negotiation, taking the posture that encouraging trade or investment is a concession. Nothing could be further from the truth. India should move to systematically lower tariff barriers and eliminate regulatory barriers to trade and investment because doing so will make all Indians better-off. The adjustment process will undoubtedly be painful, but embracing globalization is the only proven way to increase the incomes of all citizens, not just the politically favored.

Comment

Murli Manohar Deora
Member of Parliament, India

Since its introduction in 1991, economic reform in India has come a long way. A primary feature of it has been the liberalization of trade and investment policies with the objective of hastening the process of economic globalization. There is however, unhappiness still, both within and outside, about the degree of liberalization. For instance, there are complaints about India's tariff rates, procedural bottlenecks to investment, limited access to the services market, etc. What is often not appreciated by the reform-hungry, unhappy lot is that in every economy, liberalization has to be a gradual process, and that it must be consistent with the aspirations of the people. Liberalization is not the end, but only a means to a larger end, which is development.

The way India views development is that it is a situation where opportunities are created for people and liberalization the means to empowering people, so that they can access opportunities. If liberalization does not bring development, it would bring crisis, as in Latin America.

Globalization falls into the same context. Globalization is an opportunity for nationals of one country to benefit from developments elsewhere through cross-border flows of not just goods, services and capital but also knowledge, ideas, technology etc. The pitfalls of globalization, in its narrow sense, have to be avoided if globalization has to benefit all. It is the imperative of managed globalization that guides India's trade and investment policies. Look at it the other way as well. It is the properly-directed trade and investment policies that would help India to manage globalization and enable India to achieve its national goals.

The results of Election 2004 in India further vindicate this point. People did not vote for the status quo. They voted for a betterment of life and for equitable distribution of the benefits of growth. The people have voted for reform with a human face. People understand that growth is not possible without liberalization, but they also want a kind of growth that can remove poverty by generating employment opportunities. The question here is simple: how to make trade and investment policies serve these ends i.e. removing poverty and generating employment through trade and investment. The Indian government believes this is very much an attainable goal.

To a large extent, India's liberalization has been self-determined and unilateral. Its actual tariffs, be it for agricultural commodities or industrial products, are much less than our bound tariffs, and India has been consistently lowering tariffs not because it is under external pressure, but because it feels the need to do it. At the same time, the pace of reduction is dependent on what the economy and its stakeholders can bear. Stakeholders should not be made to perceive liberalization as a threat. In the same way, while India engages in a multilateral forum like WTO, India is opposed to multilateral rules on investment and competition policy. India has unilaterally liberalized FDI policy and has taken steps to introduce an Act on competition policy. India also encourages bilateral routes to investment liberalization and has over 40 bilateral investment treaties. Five broad dimensions of India's globalization strategy, in the context of the above background, can be reiterated as follows.

Trade Policy Liberalization

No physical controls on imports, gradual dismantling of fiscal controls, compatibility with multilateral rules, export thrust sans WTO-prohibited subsidies, constant focus on trade facilitation, etc., are some of the hallmarks of our trade policy.

However, India is also moving ahead on the road to sectoral tariff liberalization. India is signatory to ITA II for elimination of tariffs on IT products by 2005. It is mainly on agricultural products that the government has serious reservations on substantial reduction of tariffs, in view of food security concerns of over 650 million farmers who cannot be exposed to the volatilities of global commodity prices and the evils of high subsidies in the advanced countries.

Other than tariff measures, the government does not resort to non-tariff barriers as protectionist measures. With continuous and ongoing efforts to simplify trade procedures, there is an effort to dismantle non-tariff barriers that currently hurt our exports more than imports.

Regionalism

India has always been a strong advocate of multilateralism, and remains committed to its position as a founding member of GATT/WTO. However, in keeping with global trends, it is also looking at strategic engagements on a regional basis, especially when regionalism is of the open type. Previous governments had opted for comprehensive economic cooperation agreements with Sri Lanka (South Asian Free Trade Area (SAFTA)); Thailand, Myanmar, Bhutan, Nepal and Sri Lanka (BIMST–EC FTA); Singapore (Comprehensive Economic Cooperation Agreement); and, Thailand and ASEAN (FTAs).

As can be seen, the thinking is clear. India is keen on integrating its economy with (i) South Asia and (ii) fast-moving economies of Southeast/East Asia, as part of its globalization strategy. For India, globalization has to begin with a continentalization of its economy. Towards this end, we are also seeking a closer partnership with China. Of course, we believe that all these have to be within the bounds of WTO (GATT Article XXIV) guidelines. Also, unlike many countries, we believe that regionalism is not, and must not be, a substitute for multilateralism.

Multilateralism

Accordingly, every country has a responsibility towards strengthening multilateralism and towards the World Trade Organization. WTO provides the much desired checks and balances, and promotes a kind of global trading environment that suits everyone.

India is committed to the success of the Doha round of negotiations, where interest in development concerns is an essential part of negotiations. India takes part in the negotiations to ensure that the interest of all is promoted. But liberalization and/or market opening by developing countries would be of little help without a matching commitment to market access from the developed countries. India believes that there is scope for reduction of barriers to trade within the developing countries. The essence of multilateral liberalization in an unequal world economy is that each economy contributes to it according to their individual capacities. India aims for sustainable liberalization.

Investment Liberalization

This government recognizes the imperative of liberalizing investment flows and providing a conducive environment to foreign investors. It wants foreign investors to build long-term stakes in the Indian economy and make profits while doing business in India. Various surveys have shown that foreign investors in India are gradually realizing better returns from their Indian operations.

If the output is not large enough, it is because the scale of business is not large. India wants foreign investors to expand their operations. In the manufacturing sector, where more investments are needed, there are not many policy hurdles.

Similarly, the government has liberalized investments (with respect to portfolio investments) in the capital market, with a full facility for capital account convertibility. Foreign investment in services is in the process of liberalization on a unilateral basis, and substantial liberalization has already been undertaken in the financial sector.

However, in order to continue with the liberalization in services, India needs reciprocal commitments on liberalization of market access for its skilled people. The incidents of backlash against outsourcing in the world's richest economy makes the government hesitant about further liberalization of the services market. While India unilaterally liberalizes, and are committed to doing so, it needs reciprocity in liberalization in order to sustain the process.

Investments Abroad

The last aspect of India's approach to globalization lies in encouraging Indian investments abroad. The trend of Indian companies investing abroad is not new. It goes back to the 1960s, when global FDI flows had virtually come to a halt. Today, Indian companies are better-equipped in terms of expertise, experience and resources. The government would like to encourage Indian companies to become Indian multinational corporations. A couple of them have already done it. Their stocks are listed abroad and have traded well.

India is steadily marking her presence in the globalizing world economy. One obvious sign of it is that the performance of its economy is very much dependent on the performance of the world economy. A crash in the global stock markets would affect India's stock markets. The fortunes of Indian investors are linked to those of investors elsewhere. When the world economy is in good shape, exports grow 15-20% a year. India, therefore, has a natural stake in globalization and its success.

The trouble with globalization is that, when any part of the world economy is not functioning, the entire global economy is disturbed. Worse still, it creates distortions all over. India has experienced it several times ever since the mid-1980s. The world economy is a hotbed of distortions and dissatisfactions around it are plentiful. An indication of this was given in Cancun, the venue for the WTO's Fifth Ministerial. The single most important message that has come out clearly is this: the time has arrived for really `meaningful liberalization'.

In Cancun, we saw collective resistance to several Singapore issues. To my knowledge, most developing countries, and especially the least developed among them, have been pursuing most of the liberal trade and FDI policies. I begin to wonder, why then was there so much resistance to the Singapore issues? I found the answer to this in UNCTAD's *Least Developed Countries Report 2004*, which opened with two significant observations:

1) 'The incidence of poverty increased unambiguously in those economies that adopted the most open trade regimes and in those that continued with the most closed regimes'.
2) 'The greatest improvement was observed in those [economies] which opened up [only] moderately…[rather] than those which opened up the most'.

I am sure many developing countries will say the same thing about their economies. The message is clear: it is the middle path that one should tread. No economy is opposed to globalization, but this does not mean that every economy should pursue it at the same speed. The speed of liberalization is a prerogative of the respective governments, and it cannot be dictated by the forces exogenous to the system.

Indian economists and activists are often of the view that in India, people cannot agree on what is best for the country and its huge population.

In the context of globalization global investors and corporations often pronounce judgements on the countries they want to invest in and then release a certain set of investors' ratings.

In a theater, the actors are not the directors. But this, unfortunately, is what is happening in the theater of globalization. Let it not be like this.

ENERGY

Scenario

V. Raghuraman
Advisor, Confederation of Indian Industry

Energy is the prime mover of economic growth and is vital to the sustenance of a modern economy. India ranks sixth in the world in terms of total energy consumption and needs to accelerate the development of the sector to meet its growth aspirations. However, development of the Indian energy sector has been constrained by capital, technology, environment and security issues arising from internal and external conditions.

Although India is rich in coal and abundantly endowed with renewable energy in the form of solar, wind, hydel and bio-energy, its hydrocarbon reserves are really small (0.4% of the world's reserves). India is a net importer of energy with more than 25% of primary energy needs being met through imports. If we look at the pattern of energy production, coal and oil account for 52% and 33% respectively, with natural gas, hydro and nuclear contributing to the balance.

The Indian energy sector has been structurally managed by five different ministries, and power, for example, is a concurrent subject of both the center and states. Although reforms in the energy sector are underway, the pace of reform is different in the sub-sectors of power, coal, oil, gas and renewables. There are other issues to deal with, such as low per capita energy consumption, skewed distribution of the primary energy sources, high energy intensity, energy subsidy and realization of user charges.

The energy scenario of India needs to be viewed in this background and policy initiatives must essentially aim at long-term availability of energy from sources that are accessible and affordable. This can then push the Indian economy forward on its desired higher growth trajectory and yet maintain environmental responsibility.

Special attention needs to be paid to the power sector to propel economic growth. Despite significant growth in terms of technological sophistication and capacity addition, the sector has been suffering from financial sickness and supply constraints. The enactment of the Electricity Act is clearly a step in the right direction in taking the sector from 'bankruptcy to bankability' so as to attract investment from the capital market and to supply quality power at affordable prices.

The passing of the Electricity Act has led to a substantial surge in investments in the sector. Investments in the power sector surged 16.2% as compared to 4% in fiscal year 2002/03, and accounted for a third of all project investments as at March 2004. The surge in power projects also resulted in investments in a large number of captive coal mining projects and coal washeries as supporting ventures to power projects. Fiscal year 2003/04 has also recorded a whopping reduction of over Rs80 billion in SEB losses, and as many as 11 states have reduced losses in the last fiscal year.

OPTIMISTIC SCENARIO

The establishment of market-determined prices for energy is critical if financing is to be made available for maintaining facilities, establishing new capacity in the energy sector and supporting effective transport mechanisms to move energy to users in a sustainable manner. Energy subsidies in India, which is approximately 1% of national income, lead to energy-intensive economic structures and technologies, and wasteful management practices.

According to a McKinsey & Company study, at present, the average productivity of transmission and distribution (T&D) in India is only 4%, while the best-practice case is 33%. It could be possible to improve it to 42% by reducing theft and manpower, by putting in place 100% metering, and employing energy-efficient transformers, capacitors and end-use appliances. By improving efficiency in power generation, and removing transmission bottlenecks and distribution breakdowns, India could substantially bring down new capacity addition requirements. A recent World Bank report also shows that Indian industry has the potential to save 20 to 30% of total energy consumption.

Energy conservation in India is gaining momentum. The Energy Conservation Act, enacted in 2001, spells out the roadmap for the country to move up the energy efficiency ladder and is set to radically change the approach towards energy conservation efforts. The Energy Conservation Act aims to focus on the enormous potential in adopting energy-efficient measures in various sectors of the economy in order to reduce overall energy consumption.

Power trading in India is in a nascent stage, and is characterized by low volumes and evolving commercial mechanisms. The provision of non-discriminatory open access in the Electricity Act is likely to facilitate trading. The proposed Petroleum Regulatory Board Bill and Gas Pipeline policy show the government's determination towards strengthening reforms of the energy sector.

For the smooth operation of the energy sector, there should be a well-established institutional framework consisting of regulatory agencies, the rules and regulations of the sector and policy guidelines. The regulatory agency should have members with international experience, political independence, accountability, autonomy and expertise on technology, economics, law and accounting.

Since the energy sector in India is governed by several ministries, there is a need for coordination and integration among these ministries. In such a situation, PMO-type initiatives to coordinate and integrate all the ministries associated with the 'energy value chain' are needed. It is also important to explore the possibilities of grouping these ministries under a 'common regulatory framework'.

In 2002/03, energy and peak load shortages were 8.8% and 12.2% respectively. As GDP growth accelerates to an ambitious 10%, the shortage of power will become more severe. Under such circumstances, an imaginative repositioning of the power sector is needed. The aim is to double the existing capacity in order to meet the higher growth trajectory and also accomplish the targeted mission of 'Power for All', by 2012.

Since India has vast coal reserves, it is expected that power generation from coal will continue in future. But in order to achieve higher thermodynamic efficiency, minimize environmental impact and pursue cost-effective utilization of high-ash Indian coal, emphasis should be given to clean coal technologies like ultra supercritical and fluidized bed combustion technologies, integrated gasification combustion cycles

(IGCC), underground coal gasification etc. The Clean Development Mechanism (CDM), adopted in the Kyoto Protocol, can be used to finance such projects.

In India, only 15% of hydro potentials has been harnessed and 7% is under various stages of development. The utilization of hydropower in India is much lower than some other countries, such as Norway (58%), Canada (41%) and Brazil (31%). The Ministry of Power (MoP) has outlined an ambitious target of adding 50,000 MW hydro capacity by the next decade. This capacity addition will be over and above the targeted capacity addition of 14,000 MW during the 10th Five-Year Plan period. A total of 162 hydel projects in 16 states have been identified for the preparation of a preliminary feasibility report by the Central Electricity Authority (CEA). The initiative will require funds amounting to Rs2,250 billion with an equity of Rs700 billion and debt of Rs1,550 billion. It has been suggested that the equity component be met by way of gross budgetary support of Rs200 billion each during the 10th and 11th Five-Year Plan periods. For the rest of the equity, the central government proposes to levy a cess of 3 paise on every unit of power generated over the next 10 years.

In India, gas production comes mostly from the Western offshore area. Recently, Reliance and Cairn have reported seven trillion cubic feet and one trillion cubic feet of gas finds from two blocks in the Krishna-Godawari Basin. Similar gas potential is also expected on the West Coast.

But the new domestic gas finds or other such discoveries in the future would not eliminate the prospect of importing piped gas or liquefied natural gas (LNG). Ample opportunities exist for an inter-country, high-pressure gas pipeline, as it is the most cost-effective way of importing gas from the Middle East, Central Asia and neighboring countries like Bangladesh and Myanmar.

Importing LNG is more capital-intensive than piped gas. However, in order to avoid the geopolitical uncertainty associated with the import of piped gas through Pakistan, India has opted for the import of costlier liquefied LNG from the North Field of Qatar by LNG tankers. India's first five-million-ton capacity LNG terminal at Dahej, constructed by public sector oil company consortium Petronet LNG Ltd. (PLL), is now fully operational. PLL has signed an agreement with RasGas of Qatar to purchase LNG at a fixed price equivalent to $20 a barrel for 25 years. The price translates into a FOB price of $2.79 per million BTU (British thermal unit).

However, the price of around $3.6 per mmbtu by PLL has so far been unacceptable to consumers. Most of the user industries are hoping for a better price from rival gas companies like Shell (Hazira LNG project), as well as natural gas which is being promised by Reliance Industries.

In terms of Long Range Marginal Cost (LRMC) advantages, nuclear power is a genuine economic option for power supply at locations far remote from coal reserves, particularly if hydel sources are not available in the vicinity. The cost of nuclear power is comparable to that of coal-based power at locations that are 1,000 km away from the coal pit-heads. Although the present share of nuclear power is only 2.59% (2,720 MW) of the total installed capacity, the Vision 2020 of the Department of Atomic Energy envisages a cumulative installed capacity of 20,000 MW.

India is planning to add about 12,000 MW power-generating capacity from renewables by the end of the 11th Plan (2007-2012) period. Almost half of it will come from wind, 3,500 MW from biomass and 2,000 MW from small hydro. Renewables are capable of meeting the energy needs of rural areas in an economically efficient manner.

There exists a close linkage between carbon trading and the development of the renewable energy market. Analysis shows that renewable energy technologies are one of the low-cost options for carbon mitigation. In the next decade, carbon trading could be one of the instruments which can push renewable energy technology.

South Asia, which includes countries like Bangladesh, India, Nepal, Sri Lanka, Maldives and Bhutan, is endowed with untapped energy resources but their development, efficient distribution and utilization will require cooperation and trading among the countries.

Although some exchange of electricity already occurs among Nepal, Bhutan and India, multilateral cooperation to develop and exchange energy resources will have far-reaching economic and security benefits. India can benefit from electricity and gas imports from neighboring countries as it fosters its development aspirations; Bangladesh, Nepal, Bhutan and Myanmar could realize significant economic benefits from the development and export of hydroelectric power and natural gas; and Pakistan could benefit from electricity export from an independent power producer.

The transportation of gas using pipelines via Pakistan is the most cost-effective way of importing gas from the Middle East and Central Asia to India. Pipelines could be incentives for the building of good political relations between India and Pakistan as gas pipelines would help Pakistan procure substantial transit fees as well as an assured gas supply. It has been estimated that Pakistan would obtain a total estimated income of $14 billion over 30 years, out of which $8 billion would be the transit fee that Iran has offered the country, $1 billion would be collected in taxes and $5 billion in energy cost savings.

India's ever-increasing import dependence on oil gives rise to oil security concerns. The demand for gas is also growing at a faster rate and due to limited domestic reserves, the country would also have to be dependent on gas imports. Middle Eastern countries are the largest source of oil/gas imports but the region is susceptible to disturbances and there may be disruptions in supply. The choices available for increasing oil security may include the enhancement of strategic oil/gas reserves, investments in oil equity abroad, the enhancement of domestic oil/gas reserves through accelerated exploration, diversification of sources of oil/gas imports (instead of relying solely on the Middle East region), and the building of adequate oil and gas transfer infrastructure to meet future demand.

The issues related to India's energy security need to be revisited in a comprehensive manner in order for optimal utilization of indigenous and externally traded energy sources to meet demand at affordable prices.

WORST-CASE SCENARIO

Highly unlikely worst possible situations could be summarized as:

- Huge demand-supply gap because of poor vision and distortionary policies
- Slow pace of reform due to a lack of understanding of the ground realities, lack of political will and vested political interests
- Poorly managed energy subsidy issues and rationalization of user charges

- Lack of private sector investment in resource-starved energy sector
- Lack of infrastructure development for energy transportation and distribution
- Poor hydro and nuclear capacity additions due to lack of investments and opposition from NGOs and environmental lobbies
- Restricted captive power policy by the states on evacuation, wheeling, tariffs and banking
- Low yields of indigenous oil fields and larger dependence on oil import
- Restricted cross-border energy trading due to geopolitical problems
- Poor power evacuation facilities
- Environmental pollution due to market failure

CONCLUSION

Energy consumption in India is a stimulus for economic growth. The supply-constrained sub-optimal consumption of commercial energy would adversely affect the productive sectors, which in turn would hamper economic growth. India, thus, needs novel initiatives to promote the diversification of its energy portfolio, for integrated resource planning, and energy conservation and efficiency improvement programs, in order to achieve sustainable development.

Comment

N.K. Singh
Chairman, Indian Institute for Management and Development, India

OVERVIEW

The development of an efficient and adequate energy supply is important for the achievement of economic growth potential in India. Although the 10th Plan has projected a GDP growth rate of 8% in India, the growth rate of demand for energy is estimated to be lower than this. This is due to lower aggregate energy intensity, which is partly because of increased energy efficiency measures, as well as the gradual shift to less energy-intensive economic activities like IT.

The objective of reaching 8% GDP growth rate over the period of the Plan would require wider policy reforms that take into account the changing global scenario and that is targeted at achieving an optimal fuel mix. The accepted paradigm on energy management is undergoing significant changes not only in terms of new research and development on energy sources, but also as a consequence of increased integration of the global trading system.

Per capita electricity consumption in India is one of the lowest when compared to the international average and other developing countries. Regional variation shows greater disparities. The northeastern region has the lowest consumption of 106 kWh as compared to the 530 kWh for the western region followed by 470 kWh in the southern, 324 kWh in the northern and 205 kWh in the eastern region. The higher levels of per capita consumption in some of the abovementioned regions could be because of greater levels of industrialization in those regions, as well as the state government's stated policy objectives to extend the T&D network to all rural areas to ensure load growth and overall economic development.

Over the years, India's energy sector has received priority in terms of financial allocation of the resources of the Plan. Its share of resources in the overall Plan rose from 15% from the 3rd Five-Year Plan (1961-66) to nearly 27% in 1999/2000. In the 10th Plan, the share of resources in the

Plan is about 24% only. Despite significant sectoral growth, the supply of energy from various sources has fallen short of demand, hence adversely affecting growth in other sectors of the economy.

There has been a substantial addition to generation capacity from a mere 1,363 MW at the time of independence to over about 105,000 MW as on 31 March, 2002. This volume includes 26,260 MW of hydropower which accounts for 25% of total installed capacity. Of this, the State Electricity Boards (SEBs) have an installed capacity of 62,245 MW, and the central power sector undertakings have 31,605 MW, including 2,720 MW of nuclear power. The private sector has an installed capacity of 11,066 MW. In terms of installed capacity of 105,000 MW in the utilities and another 25,000 MW in captive capacity, only China with 330 GW and Russia 200 GW have bigger capacity, among the developing countries. India's installed capacity is more than double that of Korea and about eight times that of the Philippines.

In terms of the fuel mix (excluding captive), thermal, hydro and nuclear capacities account for 72%, 25.03% and 2.59% respectively, at the end of March 2002. Apart from conventional sources, about 3% of energy needs are also met by non-conventional sources such as wind power, biomass, small hydro and solar power etc. In spite of the abovementioned growth in power, the availability has not been able to keep pace with the growth in demand. The overall peak deficit has been about 12.2% and base energy deficit was about 8.8% at the end of March 2003. It is estimated that the country needs to create an additional capacity of 100,000 MW by the end of 10 years to meet the growing demand for power.

While the SEBs have performed well in generation and transmission, distribution, however, remains as the weakest link, and suffers from various problems. The root of the problem lies in the gap between user charges and cost of supply. Despite graduated hikes in user charges, the gap between cost of supply and average tariff per unit of electricity produced has actually worsened from a level of 23 paise in 1992/93 to about 110 paise in 2001/02. Revenues dropped from 82% of costs in 1992/93 to 69% in 2001/02. The financial health of SEBs has been adversely affected, the sector's ability to invest has been curbed and private investments have been discouraged. The total commercial losses of the SEBs increased from Rs4,117 crores in 1991/92 to Rs27,000 crores in 2001/02. The net subsidy of Rs5,404 crores on agriculture and domestic sectors in 1991/92 has increased substantially to about Rs26,600 crores in 2001/02.

All these factors have contributed to the SEBs' substantial losses, and they were thus unable to provide much-needed generation capacity, improvements in T&D and qualitative services to the consumers. It was under these circumstances that the government decided to undertake major reforms in the power sector.

POWER REFORMS

Power sector reforms were initiated in 1991 to encourage competition in each subset of the sector—generation, transmission and distribution. The Central Electricity Regulatory Commission (CERC) was set up at the national level in 1997 and State Electricity Regulatory Commissions (SERCs) have now been set up in 22 states, 13 of which have issued tariff orders so far. Private participation in power transmission is now allowed with the enactment of the Electricity Laws (Amendment) Act in 1998. The Indian Electricity Grid Code was established in January 2000 by the CERC to ensure grid discipline for individual players in the T&D sector. The Availability-Based Tariff Order of January 2000 by the CERC is expected to encourage reliability and efficiency in generation.

The Electricity Bill, originally drafted in 2001, was recently passed by the parliament in 2003. It would replace the three existing laws on electricity, i.e. the Indian Electricity Act, 1910; the Electricity (Supply) Act, 1948; and the Electricity Regulatory Commission Act, 1998. It recognizes the trading of power as a distinct activity and provides a legal framework for enabling reforms and restructuring of the power sector. Already, SEBs in nine states have been unbundled/corporatized. The newly set-up distribution companies are expected to emulate the successes of private sector distribution in Mumbai, Kolkata and Ahmedabad, and ensure effective enforcement of user charges. The Energy Conservation Act 2001 was enacted to provide for efficient use of energy and its conservation. The Bureau of Energy Efficiency (BEE) was set up and the Honorable Prime Minister released its action plan on 23 August, 2002.

The Accelerated Power Development Program (APDP), initiated in 2000/01 and subsequently modified as Accelerated Power Development and Reforms Program (APDRP) with an outlay of Rs3,500 crores, has been designed to assist reforms in the distribution sector. It aims at providing 100% metering, energy audits, replacements of distribution transformers, and IT solutions relating to power flow at critical points to ensure accountability at all levels. The APDRP also provides financial incentives to the states to reduce the gap between unit cost of supply and revenue realization. The Ministry of Power has already signed memoranda of understanding (MoU) with 25 states to undertake reforms in a time-bound manner.

On the issue of outstanding SEB dues to Central Public Sector Units (PSUs), and dues from Central PSUs to State Power Utilities, the Ahluwalia Expert Group, constituted by the Ministry of Power in 2001, has designed a securitization scheme for a one-time settlement of the approximately Rs420 billion payable by SEBs to Central Government PSUs as on 30 September, 2001 after writing off Rs96 billion.

In line with this, a tripartite agreement was signed recently in March 2003 between the Ministry of Power, State Governments and the Reserve Bank of India (RBI). Bonds worth Rs21,211.50 crores from 17 states have already been floated by RBI. RBI proposes floating the bonds for the balance amount of Rs10,800 crores in the second trench, probably by the end of September 2003.

However, a great deal of work remains to be done, particularly at the state level. The reform template recently put forward by the Ministry of Power's Expert Committee on State Specific Reforms could be helpful in making further progress. Some of the policy initiatives already taken or are required in the power sector are:

- Rationalizing power tariffs and making the tariff-setting process transparent
- Reflecting cost of service in the tariffs and transferring all subsidies explicitly to state budgets
- Improving efficiency in all the three segments viz. generation, transmission and distribution, either by creating separate profit centers with full accountability within the vertically integrated structure, or

unbundling SEBs into generation, transmission and distribution entities or through other models of reform, depending on the choice of the state government
- Encouraging competition and private participation in each element of the electricity value chain
- Instituting open access by separating the carriage (transmission and distribution network) from the content (power and energy), thereby enabling customers to source their requirements from the most efficient source (completed)
- Redesigning APDP as APDRP with provisions for release of funds linked to the achievement of certain parameters and benchmarks (completed)
- Actively promote R&D on fast breeder reactors and thorium-based technologies for nuclear power
- Energy conservation and demand-side management

LONG-TERM ENERGY APPROACH

India's energy use is mostly based on fossil fuels. Although the country has significant coal and hydro resource potential, it is relatively poor in oil and gas resources. As a result, it has to depend on imports to meet its energy needs.

The development model followed so far to meet the energy requirements of the human population, which has an excessive dependence on fossil fuel resources such as coal, oil and natural gas, is not only unsustainable in the long run, but it also has an adverse impact on the environment and ecology, and disastrous consequences to natural resources. It is against this backdrop that non-conventional or renewable sources of energy are suggested to achieve the goal of sustainable development.

However, in the long term, development of the power sector would largely depend on the development of the energy sources, and a coordinated and fast-paced development of these sources is a 'sine qua non' for power development. Some of the policy initiatives required in the sector are stated as follows.

Petroleum Sector

Oil accounts for about 35% of the total primary energy supply in India today. While the demand for petroleum products has risen substantially, the Indian upstream sector has lagged behind, raising concern for oil security in the country.

Today, 70% of the total demand for petroleum products is met through imports. Domestic crude oil meets only 30% of total requirements. The policy initiatives for the oil sector include:

- deregulation of the petroleum sector with the dismantling of APM (completed)
- establishment of a regulatory authority for the petroleum sector, which also includes natural gas
- restructuring/disinvestment of oil and gas PSUs on a selective basis
- oil security through accelerated exploration activities, diversification of sources, securing equity oil abroad and strategic storage of oil
- development of alternative fuels such as CBM, MS-Ethanol blend and gas hydrates
- benchmarking of the hydrocarbon sector to international levels
- facilitating a greener and cleaner environment in the country by setting emission norms and product quality specifications

Coal Sector

There are abundant reserves of coal in India, and at current production rates, domestic coal would last over 200 years. Coal accounts for 56% of total primary energy for commercial uses in the country, with over 90% of the requirement met by domestic coal. However, increasingly, domestic coal is being crowded out by imported coal and natural gas. In view of this, the following strategies are imperative to increase the efficiency in the sector:

- continuation of the reform process and facilitation of private sector participation in commercial coal mining, with a view to gaining access to the latest technologies and to raising competitiveness through competition
- restructuring of the coal sector by providing more autonomy to individual coal-producing companies in order to promote

competitiveness, revive loss-making coal companies and encourage/ discourage disinvestments of the selected coal PSUs
- setting up of a regulatory authority for resolving disputes and allocation of coal blocks both for exploration and exploitation
- intensification of exploration activities and upgrades of coal reserves to the proven and recoverable category in terms of energy security
- improvement of environmental aspects and promotion of clean coal technologies—beneficiation of non-coking coal for power generation; development of coal bed methane; carbon dioxide sequestration; coal gasification; integrated gas combined cycle (IGCC) and fluidized bed combustion (FBC) route of power generation; and development of slurry transportation etc.

Renewables (including small hydro)

The share of renewable sources of energy in the world is progressively increasing. These resources are especially used for distributed generation and to meet the requirements of remote/difficult-to-access areas.

In India too, the share of renewables in total power generation capacity has been increasing gradually over the last few years. These achievements, however, are dwarfed by the total potential available in the country. The gross wind power potential has been estimated at 45,000 MW and the potential from small hydro projects is estimated at about 15,000 MW. A potential of 16,000 MW (conservative estimate) of power from surplus/ distributed biomass materials has also been estimated. The following steps need to be taken to encourage renewable sources in the country:

- identify remote areas where power supply from the conventional grid will be prohibitively expensive and make it a priority to provide off-grid supply from renewables for these areas. Formulate enabling provisions for integrated generation and distribution of off-grid energy supply by, for instance:
    * conducting a comprehensive review of program objectives, achievements to date, and the efficacious use of funds, and,
    * clarifying the framework for supply to main grid by providing regulatory certainty on tariff, off-take agreements, and direct/ contracted sale of bulk users

- encourage private sector investments in renewable energy sources by promoting a bidding process for available subsidies. Award contracts to private entrepreneurs who provide maximum benefits with the lowest amount of subsidies.

POSSIBLE DIRECTIONS FOR ALTERNATIVE FOCUS OF REFORMS

The last 10 years have seen intensive discussion on power sector reforms. The policy framework is now in place to actually implement them. The ultimate vision of the power sector, embedded in the Electricity Act 2003, is that of a fully competitive sector, with competition at every level possible, so as to ensure that there is ever-increasing drive for efficiency and cost reduction.

The success of reforms in India will depend critically upon the existence of some sort of restraining or disciplining mechanism in the sector. Without this, current efforts will likely result in a transition from inefficient public ownership to aggressive profit-making monopolies or oligarchies.

In principle, such a mechanism should be strong, independent and effective. The focus of reforms during the transitional phase should be on improving governance; introducing incentive mechanisms; meeting energy service needs instead of merely attracting investments for centralized capacity addition; and addressing upfront the issues that are unlikely to be taken care of by the private sector, such as access, strategic and import dependence, and other social and environmental issues.

Comment

Mukesh Ambani
Chairman, Reliance Industries Limited and Chairman, IPCL

With over 75 million hectares of forest area and over 70% of total population rural at the time of independence, the share of non-commercial sources like firewood, dung cake and agricultural waste in India's energy consumption was a staggering 70%. The demographic shifts over the past 50 years have resulted in a reversal of this proportion, and today, India consumes 325 million tons of oil equivalent (MTOE) and is the world's sixth largest consumer of commercial primary energy. In the process, commercial energy consumption has increased more than tenfold during this shift away from non-commercial energy. Despite this, the per capita consumption, at a little over 300 kg, remains one of the lowest in the world and India continues to remain energy-deficient. Further, a large population still does not have access to commercial energy.

Due to coal being cheap and locally available, India's commercial energy consumption is heavily skewed towards coal, and coal accounts for 55% of total consumption. This is, however, still lower than in China, where coal accounts for nearly 70% of total consumption. Oil accounts for 31% of India's primary energy consumption, natural gas 8%, hydro 5% and nuclear 1%. Natural gas is expected to be the fastest-growing fuel in India in the coming years, with its share expected to reach the world average level of about 24% within the next 10-15 years, from 8% today.

India's heavy dependence on energy imports in the past was due to limited resources of oil and natural gas on one hand, and rapidly increasing demand on the other. The last few years have even seen coal being imported.

The elasticity of energy consumption with respect to GDP has steadily declined over the years, from about 1.5 in the 1970s, to 1.2 in the 1980s, and to unity in the 1990s. While a few of the past trends do not reflect the genuine demand growth but merely the growth of actual availability, efficiency gains have certainly been achieved and this has lowered the demand elasticity. There is, however, considerable scope for further improvements and management initiatives, both on the demand side and on the supply side.

The principles of pricing adopted for energy products have greatly influenced the pattern of energy growth in the country in the past. While some of these policy initiatives were essential in the early stages of development, their shortcomings and their adverse economic implications like inefficient resource allocation, lack of end-use efficiencies, and lack of viability and financial autonomy of the sector, have now been identified and attempts are well underway to make the transition to a market-based pricing system as opposed to the administered pricing system.

The reforms are in various stages of implementation in each of the sub-sectors, and in the sectors where they have progressed significantly, the benefits are already clearly visible, in the form of increased investment flows, availability of products and services, improved quality, wider consumer choices and lower end-use prices. Thus, the country is on the right track to make the energy sector truly vibrant so that it can efficiently meet the ever-growing demands that would result from the double-digit economic growth rates, which India is now pursuing.

Some of the recent large-scale discoveries of natural gas reserves in India, and increasing efforts in harnessing coal bed methane and prospecting natural gas hydrates are further supporting the optimism. Increased use of natural gas in India in the coming decades will clearly help the country achieve the popularly known 3E goals in the energy sector—economic efficiency, environment protection and energy security—simultaneously.

COAL AND LIGNITE

Commercial coal mining in India is more than two hundred years old. With reserves of about 221 billion tons, of which 84 billion tons are proven, coal is the most abundant domestic source of energy in India, and this is reflected in its share of total energy mix. Coal currently accounts for 70% of total power generation in India.

The coal industry has come a near full circle, from the nationalization of the coalmines in the early 1970s to the opening of the mining sector to private participation in 1993 for captive consumption. In the pipelines is the new Coal Mining Policy which would further open up the sector to private participation.

Current coal production in India is around 325 million tons per annum, and consumption is around 340 million tons. Coal production fell below the target during the 9th Five-Year Plan, but this did not present a serious problem, as the power generation capacity also did not expand as targeted. For the 10th Plan and beyond, it has become clear that a substantial expansion in domestic coal production is needed to support the demands from the power sector. Domestic coal now faces serious threats from imported coal and competing fuels, especially natural gas.

The target in the 10th Plan for coal demand is about 450 million tons by the terminal year, i.e. 2006/07 and production is expected to reach 405 million tons, and imports 45 million tons.

The current estimate for lignite reserves in the country is around 35 billion tons. The deposits, which are concentrated in the southern and western regions, have become important sources of energy for the states in these regions. Lignite production is targeted to double to about 55 million tons by the end of the 10th Five-Year Plan.

Coal gasification is considered as a promising technology for India, especially in view of the fact that nearly 75% of India's coal reserves are of inferior quality, with as high as 45% ash content.

India can learn from the strategy followed by the U.S. Department of Energy in the Clean Coal Technology Program. This is a successful and proven model of government and industry partnership. Demonstration plants are set up on a commercial scale on the user's premises and the government's share of the costs is refunded only upon the commercialization of the technology.

On its part, India's Council for Scientific and Industrial Research (CSIR) has recommended a three-pronged strategy for sustainable development of the energy sector through coal gasification technology. The immediate strategy is to establish coal gasification and Integrated Gasification Combined Cycle (IGCC) technologies for commercial applications. The recommended short-term strategy is to convert existing thermal plants to IGCC as they also use synthesis coal gas for the production of chemicals, fertilizers and steel. In the longer-term, strategies are to be adopted for replacing natural gas with coal gas, for establishing fuel cell technologies based on coal gas and the development of commercial plants for the conversion of coal to oil.

While these are long-term scenarios, considering that global reserves to production ratio for coal is around three times that for gas and four times that for oil, these technology developments are necessary aspects of any long-term energy planning and India has a great potential to take a lead role in these areas. With its vast pool of engineers and scientists, the country is well-positioned to be at the forefront of emerging technologies.

COAL BED METHANE (CBM)

While the global commercial Coal Bed Methane (CBM) club today comprises four countries—USA, Poland, China and Australia—, India, with estimated CBM reserves of about 1,000 BCM (approximately 35 TCF), is set to join this club in the near future. Large resources of high grade coal in the country provide ample opportunities for harnessing this source of non-conventional energy.

Aware of this potential, the government of India finalized a comprehensive CBM policy in 1997. In the first round of bidding, seven blocks were offered, of which five blocks were awarded. Contracts were signed in 2002. Additionally, two blocks were awarded in 2003 on a nomination basis. With the earlier signed block in May 2001, the total blocks awarded to date is eight.

Together, the blocks are estimated to hold CBM potential of 393 BCM, and produce about 13-14 MMSCMD. A second round of bidding has recently been announced with an offer of nine blocks.

CRUDE OIL AND PETROLEUM PRODUCTS

Oil was first struck in Digboi in the 1880s. Today, India's petroleum industry is over a century old. However, even at the time of independence, there was only one refinery in India with a capacity of just 0.25 MMTPA. At the time of nationalization (1974-95), the refining capacity in India was about 28 MMTPA.

India has made rapid strides in the petroleum sector in the last 30 years. Progress was made across the entire value chain—from exploration through refining, to distribution and marketing of petroleum products.

From a level of just 18 million tons in 1970/71, consumption of petroleum products has grown at a healthy 5.5% CAGR, crossing the 100 million ton mark in 2000-01.

During the early and mid-1990s, India's self-sufficiency in petroleum products declined gradually, leading to peak product imports of almost 20 million tons a year. However, the various steps taken by the government since the early 1990s in inviting private participation and deregulating the sector have paid rich dividends in the recent past. Where the country was once a large net importer of petroleum products, it has now become a net exporter of petroleum products, and it has significantly improved energy security and saved on valuable foreign exchange.

Between 1998/99 and 2000/01, the country's refining capacity increased 64% from about 68 MMTPA to 112 MMTPA, with Reliance's Jamnagar Refinery's 27 MMTPA accounting for the bulk of the capacity increase.

However, India's self-sufficiency in crude oil continues to slide, with stagnant domestic production at around 32 million tons and rapidly increasing demand. At current levels of about 80 million tons per annum, India depends to an extent of over 70% for its crude oil import needs.

The phased dismantling of the administered pricing mechanism, which started in April 1998, is now complete. The oil pool account has been dismantled, and marketing companies have been allowed to set the retail prices for the transportation of fuels. The subsidies on domestic LPG and public distribution kerosene have been transferred to the Union Budget, and these are to be phased out in the next few years. The government has already granted marketing rights for the transportation of fuels to the 'eligible' players.

In December 2002, GOI announced the Petroleum Product Pipeline Policy, which provides a mechanism for the common carriage of petroleum products. As stated in the policy, if a company plans to lay a pipeline originating from a port, or one that exceeds 300 km in length and originates from a refinery, it must publish its intention and allow other interested companies to take a capacity in the pipeline on a take-or-pay or other mutually agreed basis. Companies laying new pipelines are required to provide for other users at least 25% extra capacity beyond what it itself would need.

The Indian petroleum product specifications are already on par with those of many developed countries, and the specifications are being further tightened in line with global developments. In October 2003, GOI approved the Auto Fuel Policy. According to the policy, Bharat Stage II compliant fuels/vehicles and Euro III compliant fuel/vehicles will be introduced in the entire country by 1 April, 2005 and 1 April, 2010 respectively. The applicable dates in relation to compliance with Bharat Stage II and Euro III have been moved to 1 April, 2003, and 1 April, 2005, respectively for 11 Indian states. In addition, for these 11 states, it has been proposed that Euro IV compliant fuels will be introduced from 1 April, 2010, on an experimental basis.

Although there is a surplus in refining capacity vis-à-vis domestic product demand at present, this is expected to be a temporary phenomenon. *The Hydrocarbon Vision 2025 Report* forecasts that the demand for petroleum products in India will reach 370 million tons by 2025.

NATURAL GAS

Natural gas accounts for only 8% of India's primary energy consumption, against the world average of 24% and 40-45% in some of the developing countries. At about 30 BCM/year, India barely figures in the top 20 gas-consuming nations in the world.

The current low consumption of natural gas can be attributed primarily to limited gas availability in the country. India accounts for a meager 0.5% of the world's total proven gas reserves.

Although India commenced gas production from as early as 1959, India took more than 25 years after independence to strike its first major discovery when ONGC discovered oil and gas in Bombay High in 1974. It took another 28 years for the next major discovery. In 2002, Reliance Industries announced its discovery in the Krishna-Godavari Basin.

Despite the limited availability so far, the country has done well in maximizing value addition. It allocates C2/C3 fractions for petrochemicals, and C4 for extraction and marketing as LPG and then, the bulk C1 fraction is sent to power, fertilizer and other industries as well as for retail distribution.

In addition to the expected boost from domestic availability, supply is also going to get a boost through the recent commissioning of the first LNG terminal at Dahej. Dahej LNG terminal makes India the first developing country to join the LNG club. India is also well-placed to receive gas through transnational pipelines. India's strategic location gives it a unique opportunity to import gas from the west (through the Middle East and Central Asia) as well as from the east (Bangladesh and Myanmar).

Besides the conventional sources, India is also seriously pursuing unconventional technologies to increase the availability of clean fuel. To harness its vast coal reserves, efforts are directed at commercializing Coal Bed Methane Production (CBM). Two rounds of bidding for CBM blocks have been completed and the first commercial CBM production is expected to commence soon. India recognizes the potential borne by new technologies like gas hydrates and under-coal gasification. Various projects are underway for the ultimate commercialization of these technologies.

On the demand side, it is widely accepted that India has almost infinite demand at the right prices. On the other hand, there is probably virtually no demand if prices were pegged at the same levels as those of the developed countries. Various studies have confirmed huge demand potential from the conventional consuming sectors—power and fertilizer. The recent enactments of the Electricity Bill 2003 and the New Pricing Policy for the fertilizer sector would go a long way in providing further ballast to gas demand. In the longer-term, newer applications of gas in areas like domestic cooking, space heating and, cooling and transportation would also drive demand growth. The success story of CNG in Delhi and Mumbai reflects the impact of the use of clean fuel on the environment. This success story would definitely be re-written in other cities facing the nuisance of pollution. India is therefore ready to achieve aggressive demand targets, given its considerable unmet demand and unexplored new areas. With the supply side in place, the challenge would therefore be to translate these supply sources into delivering gas to the consumers at the 'right prices'.

The Indian natural gas sector is undoubtedly going to witness vibrant times ahead. While the enthusiasm is justified, the task is challenging. It calls for co-ordinated and collaborative efforts from all players across the value chain, especially in view of the fact that the gas chain is highly inflexible compared to the oil chain.

The Indian gas sector is expected to witness a lot of buoyancy in the near future. The huge deepwater discoveries on its eastern coast are expected to transform the energy security landscape of India. With exploration activities intensifying, buoyed as they are by the NELP initiative of the government, significant new discoveries can be expected in the near future. The consumption of gas, which has been supply-constrained until recently, would treble in the next four to five years. A nationwide gas network would be created to complement the increasing gas availability in the country. Both the public and the private sectors would participate in the growth of this sector, which is expected to hit double-digits. The government has taken steps in the right direction. It has worked to provide a level playing field for private sector players in terms of market access, pricing and risk-sharing arrangements. With the kind of vibrancy being witnessed in the sector, there is no reason why India cannot be amongst the top five gas-consuming countries in the world by the turn of this decade.

NATURAL GAS HYDRATES

Earth's vast deposits of natural gas hydrates hold the promise of becoming a significant new source of energy, even if a fraction of its potential is commercially tapped. The global estimates of the volumes of gas in the natural gas hydrates are mind-boggling, ranging from 30,000 TCF to as high as 49*10^6 TCF. This is against the world's current proven reserves of about 5,000 TCF. At present, gas from hydrates is produced only in Russia; however, the U.S. and Japan have taken active steps in the development of gas production from hydrates.

India is considered as a very good prospect for harnessing this source of energy. Realizing its potential, the GOI has formulated the National Gas Hydrate Program. Under this program, potential areas of gas hydrate deposits have been identified along the east and west coasts of India and in the Andaman region. The preparation of the Gas Hydrate Map of India has been completed by the National Institute of Oceanography. Efforts are underway to assess the resource potential.

India will soon be at the forefront of exploitation of this seemingly endless source of energy.

POWER SECTOR

The Indian power sector has come a long way since independence. The generation capacity in the country has increased from around 850 MW to more than 108,000 MW today. The captive generation capacity stands at another 15,000 MW. India has the world's fifth largest capacity and sixth largest consumption. Around 60% of the capacity is accounted for by coal, 10% by natural gas, 25% hydro and the rest by nuclear and renewables.

The Indian power sector is, however, still beleaguered with problems such as the poor financial health of the state electricity boards, huge shortfalls in supply, vertically-integrated monopolies, excessive cross-subsidization in tariffs and low private sector participation.

Until 1990, India had followed the model of vertically-integrated state monopolies. These monopolies were responsible for generation, transmission and distribution. Generation at the state level was complemented by central sector utilities like NTPC, NHPC and NPC. Inter-state transmission was monopolized by a centrally-owned transmission company.

However, this model ultimately suffered from operational inefficiencies and excessive political interference in the operations of the state electricity boards. Almost all the SEBs were characterized by heavy financial losses, and they then required direct subsidies from the state governments, causing hence a heavy drain on state finances.

Realizing the need for reform and restructuring of the sector in order to improve its financial health and invite private participation, India started the reform process in 1991.

The underlying objectives of the reform and restructuring process include disintegrating and unbundling vertical monopolies, corporatization and subsequent privatization of the SEBs, setting up of independent regulators at the state as well as the central levels, and increasing private sector participation across the value chain viz. generation, transmission and distribution.

Though India has a generation capacity in excess of 108,000 MW, it continues to be plagued by energy and peak shortages which then chokes the country's economic growth. According to the latest estimates, the peak deficit is 12.2% and energy deficit is 9.1%, even though the per capita consumption in the country is only around 350 kWh and less than 60% of the households have access to electricity.

To increase the availability of power, the government of India has launched the aggressive program of 'Power For All', to be achieved by 2012. This would require a near-doubling of the generation capacity—an addition of another 100,000 MW in 10 years, which is what was previously managed only after a period of 50 years. Keeping in view the importance of private sector participation in generation, the government has taken a number of policy initiatives since 1991 with a view to streamlining the procedures for early implementation of the projects. These include the two-part tariff system for IPPs, automatic approval for FDI, competitive bidding for the setting-up of power projects, and defining policies for mega power projects and liquid fuel for power generation. However, these policies have not produced the desired results and only around 6,500 MW have been commissioned by the private sector so far.

The provisions of the Electricity Act, enacted in 2003, are likely to encourage private sector participation in power generation. The key features of the Act are the provisions which would help improve the state of affairs in the sector. These include the de-licensing of generation, captive generation, opening access to transmission and distribution networks, allowing generating companies to take up distribution, classifying trading as a distinct activity, setting up state regulators in all states etc.

The Act provides attractive opportunities for private investment in the sector. Being able to sell power directly to the consumer is a huge incentive to the private sector generators.

Any increase in generation capacity has to be complemented by improvements in the financial health of the SEBs, as they would continue to be the major buyers for the medium term. Policy initiatives in this regard commenced with the adoption of the Electricity Regulatory Commission

Act in 1998 which made it mandatory for all the states to set up regulatory commissions and the union government to set up a central regulatory commission. The primary objective of the regulatory commissions has been in the rationalization of tariffs and related matters.

Another key development has been the start of the process to unbundle vertically-integrated monopolies. Several states have unbundled and corporatized SEBs with the ultimate objective of privatizing them. The first privatization process carried out in the state of Orissa was a learning experience for all the stakeholders and significant improvements were made in the privatization process for Delhi. However, barring these two states, no other state is currently ready for privatization.

Although the initial stress of the government was on increasing generation capacity, it was soon realized that the success of power sector reforms hinges on active reforms in the distribution sector. Consequently, 63 circles have been identified across the country and several key initiatives like the strengthening of the sub-distribution network, 100% metering, and establishing MIS systems to improve billing and collection have been put in place. To stimulate reform processes in the state, the government has also launched the Accelerated Power Development Program. The Program provides performance-linked fiscal support to the states, where performance is based on the achievement of specific targets in the improvement of transmission and distribution networks.

Transmission and distribution are major areas where the private sector can participate. Power trading is also a potential area. A lot of activity is expected in power trading as companies can buy power from state utilities, generating companies, IPPs, and captive generators etc., and then sell it to state utilities, licensees, bulk consumers etc., regardless of whether the buyers are in the private or public sector, in India or abroad.

Power is expected to play a crucial role in India's economic growth, both as a driver of growth and as a key input for growth in other sectors. The intensity of electricity consumption is bound to increase, as 40% of households still need facilities for access to electricity. Reform and restructuring of the sector have begun and are moving in the right direction. The effects of these efforts will become evident in the near future. The private sector is expected to play a key role as reforms make the sector attractive for investment. The commitment of the state as well as that of the central government towards reforms would be critical to achieving the desired results for the sector.

HYDRO POWER

India is endowed with an economically viable hydropower potential of almost 150,000 MW of installed capacity. At a load factor of 60%, this translates into a potential of about 84,000 MW. Of this potential, less than 20% has been developed so far, indicating sufficient scope for boosting hydropower capacity in the country. The Central Electricity Authority (CEA) has identified 56 sites for pumped storage schemes, with an aggregate installed capacity potential of 96,000 MW. In addition, there is a potential of 15,000 MW from small, mini and micro hydel schemes.

The key advantage of hydropower is in its the ability to store energy and its flexibility for use during peak load periods. Hydroelectricity is a clean source of energy and not amenable to the price volatilities of fossil fuels, particularly imported fuels, and hence is best suited for meeting the peak demand.

The share of hydro generation however has gradually fallen in India over the years. Against a desirable hydro share of 40%, the current share is only 25%, and thermal generation, which should ideally be used for base-load operations, is increasingly being used to meet peaking requirements.

NUCLEAR ENERGY

Although former American President Eisenhower is credited with the term 'atoms for peace' in his famous December 1953 speech on developing peaceful applications of nuclear energy, India can certainly be credited for demonstrating to the whole world the peaceful usage of this practically limitless energy.

India's nuclear power program is based on natural uranium in the first stage, and the abundantly available thorium resources in the subsequent stages. While India's available reserves of uranium can support a 10,000 MW–program, its thorium resources could support three times that.

The Department of Atomic Energy (DAE) has acquired full indigenous capacity in all segments of the nuclear fuel cycle, right from mining, to ore processing, fuel bundle fabrication, reprocessing of used fuel and nuclear waste management. The safety operations throughout the entire cycle are on par with international best practices and comply with those recommended by various international bodies.

India is also at the forefront of technology development in the field of nuclear energy. The fast breeder test reactor at the Indira Gandhi Centre for Atomic Research is the first fast breeder reactor of its kind in the world. Further, the design of a 500 MW–prototype reactor has approached completion and is now entering the construction phase.

Nuclear energy is expected to play a much greater role in meeting India's future power needs.

RENEWABLES

India has the distinction of being the only country in the world to have an exclusive ministry dealing with new and renewable energy sources. During the last two decades, there has been a vigorous pursuit of activities towards the development, trial and induction of a variety of renewable energy technologies.

India is endowed with abundant resources of biomass, solar and wind energy. The country already ranks fifth in the world for harnessing wind energy. Apart from these, the country also has significant potential for geothermal, ocean thermal, sea wave power and tidal power.

India is fortunate to have almost 300 clear and sunny days in a year, and solar energy is widely available in most parts of the country. The Indian solar power program has two components—thermal conversion and photovoltaic.

Considerable progress has been made in the implementation of the 140 MW–Integrated Solar Combined Cycle (ISCC) Power project in Rajasthan, which has a 35 MW–solar thermal component and a 105 MW–combined cycle component. The project is funded by the World Bank/GEF and KfW of Germany. This again is the first of its kind, and among the largest of such projects in the world.

In the past few years, several organizations have started using Solar Photovoltaic (SPV) systems for a variety of applications on a commercial basis. SPV technologies also offer a unique decentralized option for providing electricity locally. This is particularly suited to India, especially in rural areas with weak or no grid connection and in other remote locations. It has been estimated that nearly 18,000 villages in remote and difficult areas of the country cannot have access to electricity through conventional grid extension, but through systems like SPV, they can.

OUTLOOK

Energy research agencies have forecasted that India's commercial energy consumption would roughly triple and reach 1,000 million tons of oil in the next 15-20 years.

If the current proportions of the energy mix continues into future, this would be equivalent to about 550 MTOE of coal consumption or about 1,100 Mt of coal consumption; 300 million tons of oil consumption or about 6 million b/d of oil consumption; about 75 MTOE of gas consumption or about 85 BCM/year (or about 230 MMSCMD); with the remaining 75 MTOE contributed by nuclear and hydro/other renewables.

But if India is to achieve a cleaner and greener fuel mix, the share of gas in the energy mix has to at least reach current world proportions. If India targets the share of gas to reach 24% by 2020, gas consumption has to increase to about 250 MTOE or about 285 BCM/year (about 780 MMSCMD), or a near tenfold increase from the current levels.

The task of meeting India's future energy needs is gigantic. But with the concentrated and coordinated efforts of all the players, i.e. government, regulators, producers, consumers and financiers, there is justified confidence that the energy sector in India will rise to the occasion. The Indian energy sector will be able to serve energy needs seamlessly and produce energy economically for the modern Indian society of the 21st century.

INFORMATION TECHNOLOGY

Scenario

Soumitra Dutta
Professor and Dean of Executive Education, INSEAD

The Indian Information and Communications Technology (ICT) sector can be proud of its achievements over the last decade and more. Good progress has been made on many dimensions. The share of the IT market in the GDP has increased from 1.22% in 1997 to an estimated 3.15% in 2003. The size of the IT market has increased from US$5 billion to US$16.4 billion over this same time period. The success of the Indian ICT sector has also enhanced India's export performance. While software exports accounted for around 5% of India's total exports in 1997, this share is more than 20% in 2003.

What will the future look like for the Indian ICT sector? Three possible scenarios and an action agenda are detailed below.

THE LOW SCENARIO: STRUCTURAL DAMAGE

India slips from its position of global leadership in the offshoring of ICT projects and business processes. Customers move their business to alternative destinations such as China, Russia and the Philippines. There is structural damage to the Indian ICT sector with firms closing operations in the face of reduced demand. The growth rate of the Indian ICT sector slows significantly from a healthy 30-40% to the single digits. This in turn significantly retards the overall growth of the Indian economy.

The low scenario could be triggered by a range of factors linked to changes in customer demand, the geopolitical environment and the competitive landscape.

Customer Demand

The Indian ICT sector remains strongly dependent upon a few countries (primarily the USA) and sectors (primarily financial services). Indian ICT firms are unable to diversify their customer base to other regions and sectors. There is a sustained downturn in either the USA or the global financial services sector, or both. Indian ICT firms are further up the value chain and suffer from the 'bullwhip' effect—i.e. relatively small changes in demand in the downstream cause large swings in the upstream.

Alternately, there is a sustained social backlash against offshoring and the movement of jobs to India and other lower cost destinations. Anti-offshoring legislations and social opposition reduce demand for the services of Indian ICT firms. Again, small changes in demand trigger the bullwhip effect. Indian firms are forced to lay off their employees and reduce operations.

Geopolitical Environment

There are significantly increased geopolitical risks in the Indian sub-continent, caused by extended periods of internal communal riots, insurgency, or wars with neighboring countries (primarily Pakistan). Concerned for their business continuity, customers move their businesses away from India to less risky locations. Assurances by Indian business and government leaders to foreign customers fall upon deaf ears.

Competitive Landscape

Other countries, most notably China, emerge as strong competitors to India and its export business. China leads the world in the production of qualified ICT engineers. China's infrastructure is world-class and leagues ahead of India's overburdened and weak infrastructure. China's strong domestic market leads the explosive growth of the ICT services market. Chinese ICT firms improve their quality and project management processes to meet or exceed those of leading Indian firms. The increased attraction of China along multiple dimensions cause large-scale shifts of offshoring activities away from India to China (and other nations).

This is, in many ways, a 'worst-case' scenario for the future of the Indian ICT sector. Indian business and government leaders have to realize that while this low scenario is not very likely, it is certainly possible. Certain actions have to be taken to prevent this scenario from materializing.

- Indian ICT firms have to diversify their customer base, both across countries and sectors, so as to reduce over-dependence on any one or two countries/sectors. In particular, greater attention and resources have to be devoted to the development of the domestic Indian market for ICT and related services.

- India has to invest in appropriate lobbying and communication efforts in the USA and other key customer countries so as to reduce the social and legislative backlash against offshoring.
- The Indian government has to proactively reduce tensions across communities within the country and, reduce the risk of terrorism and war with neighboring countries. Increased trade links with regional countries is one way to reduce the risk of war in the region.
- The Indian government has to create a favorable business environment in order to enhance the competitiveness of the Indian ICT sector. The standards in China and other leading countries could be used as benchmarks for the development of the domestic infrastructure and regulatory environment.

THE MIDDLE SCENARIO: STEADY GROWTH

The global ICT market continues to grow at a healthy rate—especially in the domain of BPO. Market opportunity is large. There is enough room across different IT service lines for Indian and other competing firms from other nations. Explosive global growth in BPO overcomes weaknesses in traditional IT application and project outsourcing.

Leveraging their tested model of global delivery, proven competency in large-scale project execution and ability to create high quality software, Indian firms continue to enjoy healthy growth. Indian firms progressively move up the value chain by investing in the domain knowledge of their customers' products. They successfully broaden their portfolio to include higher value-adding and higher margin projects. The Indian ICT sector continues on its impressive growth rate and reaches (or exceeds) the NASSCOM revenue estimates of US$77 billion by 2008.

However, some serious concerns remain for the future. The differences across the ICT capabilities of Indian and Chinese firms are minimal and in some cases, Chinese firms are larger, better-funded and more competent in specific ICT domains. Indian firms spend most of their time and resources on foreign customers. The Indian government is unable to significantly reduce the level of regulation in different industries due to continued political infighting. Consequently, growth in the domestic Indian ICT market remains stunted. BPO projects are increasing—but margins are decreasing due to increased global competition. As the labor market tightens, the costs of Indian ICT firms increase and the cost-effectiveness of the Indian ICT sector is cast into doubt. Western customers start looking at alternative locations as costs rise in India and the sustainability of India as a leading offshoring destination is called into question. The middle scenario can be triggered by several factors.

Customer Demand

Pressure on global businesses to increase productivity and improve their returns on investments accelerates. The global IT services market continues to grow at a healthy double-digit rate. The BPO market grows rapidly due to continued pressures to reduce costs. Corporations in many markets, notably North America and Europe, aggressively move IT services and business processes offshore.

Technology Trends

The internet becomes a true global phenomenon, spreading rapidly across countries and devices (PCs, handhelds, cars, watches, etc.). E-commerce is rapidly expanding and there is increased demand for global information services. Customers are becoming increasingly comfortable with online interactions with firms. Changed customer behaviors and improved global telecommunications infrastructure are allowing the decoupling of value delivery/customer interactions and production/back-office processing.

Business Environment

The business environment in India remains supportive of the development of the ICT sector. The Indian government is gradually reducing the number of regulations for industry. Gradual reductions in tariffs facilitate the spread and adoption of ICT by businesses and individuals. Improvements are made in the infrastructure but they are inadequate to bring the overall infrastructure to world-class levels. Red tape and bureaucracy continue to hinder the smooth execution of business. No radical government action or policy change is undertaken. The overall business environment in India continues to lag behind those of the developed world and other more advanced developing nations.

This is probably the most likely scenario for the Indian ICT sector over the next five years. This is, in many ways, a good scenario in that the sector experiences steady growth and contributes to the growth of the overall Indian economy. In addition to the action agenda from the previous scenario, this scenario calls for consideration of a few additional action items.

- Indian ICT firms have to become trusted business partners of their customers. They have to move up the value chain by doing higher value-adding projects—all of which will need higher levels of domain knowledge and closer relationships with customers.
- Indian ICT firms need to build and retain world-class excellence in global project delivery and quality software development. Disciplined execution and results orientation have to be among the core values for the sector.
- The cost of doing business in India has to be reduced (such as by reducing corruption and bureaucracy) and the quality of life in Indian cities/suburbs has to be improved to attract global talent. This will require rapid and adequate investments in the overall infrastructure—roads, utilities, power etc.
- The Indian government has to support and lead the growth of the domestic ICT market. In particular, the supply of ICT graduates has to be increased to meet the expected demand from the ICT sector.

However, success in the medium term (over the next five years) for the Indian ICT sector does not guarantee it long-term success. Hence, we need to consider the next scenario and innovative leadership.

THE HIGH SCENARIO: INNOVATIVE LEADERSHIP

India has developed global excellence in selected domains of technology and/or process management, and maintains a lead in these domains over developed countries and alternative offshoring locations such as China.

The Indian ICT sector continues to move forward on its path of technology leadership. Building on its successes of the past decade, Indian firms stake out leading positions in new domains of software technology. Disruptions in technology such as web services lead to fundamental changes in computing architecture. In particular, software systems need to be redesigned as services rather than products. Firms in developed nations have little choice but to depend on their trusted ICT partners in India to develop software for the new class of application services.

Indian firms move up the value chain successfully by collaborating closely with lead customers and international governing bodies; by building competence in specific verticals; and by leveraging the large talent pool of Indian university graduates.

As core processes for many global corporations are moved to India, Indian firms develop a world-class competence not only in hosting and managing business processes but also in re-engineering business processes. Indian firms combine their software execution capabilities with deep and relevant domain knowledge.

Indian ICT firms successfully leverage China's enormous opportunities. Software centers in China not only allow firms to serve China's domestic market but also to use the country to serve as a springboard to serve Japan, Korea and other countries in the Far East.

The high scenario requires the triggers of the middle scenario and a few additional ones.

Customer Demand

Disruptive technology creates new challenges for customers. For example, web services transform software from a product to a service. This calls for a rethinking of the core software applications of organizations. The complexity of the task is enormous and it involves solving associated issues such as security management and the creation of support systems (for example, billing). Customers need help to both design the systems as services and to also rethink how these services will now interact with their customers.

The need for flexible and high quality process management—including process hosting and re-engineering skills—intensifies amongst global corporations. They seek value-adding domain-specific competence and software execution capabilities from their trusted partners.

Collective Leadership

The Indian ICT sector can see the writing on the wall. If the status quo is maintained, India will be overtaken by China in less than a decade. The realization emerges that margins will continue to decrease in BPO and rapid growth in that sector alone cannot save the day. Top management becomes aware that the Indian ICT sector's best hope for the future lies in developing and exploiting unique technological competence that cannot be matched easily. A collective leadership amongst key business and government stakeholders emerges to take the ICT sector to the next level of technological excellence.

This is the best-case scenario for the Indian ICT sector—both in terms of meeting medium-term growth goals and also for creating the basis for sustainable leadership in ICT for the longer term. In addition to the action agenda of the prior scenarios, a few additional action items emerge from this scenario.

- Indian ICT firms need to make innovation and global leadership their core strategic focus. In particular, they will have to invest in research and development to be at the leading edge of technology and business practice.
- Strong partnerships need to be nurtured across Indian ICT firms and leading Indian universities and institutes of technology. Centers of innovation have to be established to both create new knowledge and educate students on the latest developments in technology practice.
- China has to be viewed more as an opportunity and less as a threat. Indian ICT firms have to aggressively enter the Chinese ICT market to diversify domestic operational risks, to serve the domestic Chinese market and also to benefit from the unique advantages of the Chinese ICT market (such as lower-cost labor).

Leadership through Focused Innovation

The Indian ICT sector has successfully evolved over the last two decades from a low-cost offshore location to a globally recognized producer of high quality software. This is core to the global success and brand image of the Indian ICT sector today. Multinationals come to India to carry out software tasks that they would not be able to do easily in developed nations. The performance of Indian ICT firms in programming productivity, software quality and other technical metrics are frequently superior to what can be achieved in developed nations. The importance of this fact, that the Indian ICT has achieved global leadership in some key domains of technology practice, cannot be overstated.

Making this transition has not been easy for the Indian ICT sector. Like other sectors and countries that have made such a transition, this has been achieved through a combination of factors including ambition, leadership, talent and luck. However, success over the last 10 years is no guarantee of success in the future. Now is not the time to sit back and enjoy the fruits of the labor of previous years. Other countries such as China are making rapid strides in improving their own ICT capabilities and reducing their competitive gaps with India.

It is said that offense is the best form of defense. India today enjoys a position of strength in the ICT sector. India has to use its current position of strength to build the future.

Focused innovation has to be the centerpiece of this strategy for the future. This blueprint recommends that the Indian ICT sector identifies specific technology domains where it can innovate and lead the world. Indian firms cannot be leaders in everything. India is a country with limited resources and infrastructure weaknesses. Hence, focus is essential—high-value ICT domains have to be identified and India has to lead the world in this area. This blueprint recommends that the Indian ICT sector focus on innovation in the following domains:

- Software process technology: Indian firms today enjoy a leadership position in quality software practices, large-scale migration projects and global project delivery.

  However, software technology is evolving rapidly and ICT projects are becoming more demanding in performance parameters. Indian firms must continue to innovate to ensure their leadership position. They should seek to remain global leaders in software delivery.

- Software re-architecturing: Indian firms should become the software architects of choice for global businesses. Software is and will remain a dominant component of business processes and end-products. Technology discontinuities (such as web services and wireless technology) will continue to appear periodically and will require the re-architecturing of both business applications and software components of end-products. This innovation in software re-architecturing will require, in many instances, the successful development of relevant domain competence, i.e. 'front-end' knowledge to complement the 'back-end' capability in software process technology.
- Business process re-engineering: India needs to become the destination of choice for the hosting and re-engineering of core business processes. This will only happen if the BPO sector first makes a deliberate transition from being seen as a low-cost BPO destination (as is largely the case today) to a hosting source of high quality business processes. A focus on innovation is needed to ensure that Indian firms are able to instil the highest quality procedures in their BPO operations and are recognized as being able to manage the processes better than their customer firms themselves (as is the situation today in the case of software projects). Next, a powerful global competence in business process re-engineering can be derived by combining this ability to host and manage high quality core processes with leading edge capabilities in software process execution and software re-architecturing.

The blueprint recognizes that a large part of the revenue growth of the Indian ICT sector over the next five years will still be driven by the sector's strengths in the traditional domains of custom application development and application outsourcing. However, it is important that India develops a unique competence in some specific domains (as outlined above) or else Indian firms will soon be competing on margins with firms from other lower-cost countries. This is not a sustainable proposition for the longer term.

Comment

Dayanidhi Maran
Minister for Information Technology, Communication and Disinvestment

The world, as well as the Asia Pacific region, has witnessed a very rapid growth in the telecommunications sector. Tele-density levels have been climbing at rates that are truly amazing. In India too, the last decade has been an exciting journey. With a subscriber base of 80 million lines, India is currently adding more than 2 million lines per month, with a significant share coming from the private sector. It is possible to at least double the current tele-density levels of 8 over the next two years or so.

The Indian telecom sector is clearly displaying the operation of market forces of demand and supply. The sovereignty of consumers is evident as they reveal their preference for economically rational decisions.

The major policy reforms undertaken through our National Telecom Policy (1994) and the New Telecom Policy (1999) have resulted in the fastest ever expansion of the telecommunications network. In the last year, we have added nearly 22 million lines and mobile connections grew at 160%.

The entry of the private sector and mobile telephones has been the principal drivers. Tariff levels have fallen significantly, and a mechanism is in place to rationalize it further, keeping in mind prevailing trends worldwide. A separate Universal Service Obligation Fund has been created to support the funding of universal access services.

Information and communication technologies are reshaping the world and new technologies in this sector hold the great promise of enabling citizens to have better access to education, health, commerce and governance. The predominant use of telecommunications services in most of our countries has so far been voice communications. While economic and social value has been provided for voice, it has not unfortunately been so for data applications. But the major drivers of future growth in this sector are related to non-voice applications namely, data communications, value-added applications, broadband interactive services, e-services and a variety of innovative content applications tailored for different age groups and interests. Immense opportunities exist, which in turn open up a vast multitude of business opportunities for the different players.

In this context, internet and broadband access are widely recognized as catalysts for the economic and social development of the country. Not only will these contribute to economic growth but they would also lead to the development of a vast pool of skilled manpower.

Having achieved a fair degree of success in improving its tele-density figures, India is on the threshold of launching a big thrust with respect to internet and broadband access. As part of the government's commitment to universal access, we are providing High Speed Public Telecom and Info Centres (HPTIC) in all major villages, i.e. villages that have a population of 2,000 persons and above. At present, our levels of internet and broadband access are low compared to countries such as South Korea, Malaysia and China. The Telecom Regulatory Authority of India has recently made some useful recommendations in this regard and has also suggested a target of 20 million broadband subscribers and 40 million internet users by the year 2010. A policy in this regard will be crafted shortly. For the current year, the target is set at a modest target of one million lines for broadband access.

Despite the overall growth in broadband penetration, it is apparent that certain economies have enjoyed more success than others in advancing broadband adoption. Most economies are still struggling to realize nationwide broadband access principally because broadband network deployment comes with high fixed costs. Although much of the technology is available to provide broadband access on a scale matching that of fixed line telephony, for largely economic reasons, the availability of broadband has lagged behind, especially in developing countries.

In this context, there is a need to pay attention to the price component. Internet and broadband access are currently an expensive proposition for a major segment of the population which is extremely price-sensitive. Cost-effective infrastructure, including handsets, as well as reasonable tariff rates will determine the future growth of internet and broadband access in the developing countries. The benefits of access can only be realized if the usage is high and if the consumer is not inhibited by high costs. All parties with a stake have a role to play. Manufacturers, for example, need to devise solutions appropriate to lower-income regions; operators must strive to find innovative solutions to keep end-user costs down.

Another constraint is in terms of establishing the technical conditions for making internet and broadband services available in all languages. There are issues in terms of the coding of scripts into computer format and also for the scripts to be used in the Uniform Resource Locater (URL). As William Butler Yeats pointed out, we must "think like a wise man but communicate in the language of the people".

A security network is an absolute sine qua non for the development of broadband facilities, particularly in the context of e-commerce. There is a need to provide for a secure and hassle-free environment.

Some countries in the Asia Pacific region have made remarkable progress in the provision of broadband services at affordable prices. The mobile telecommunication systems for providing multimedia usage via high-speed networks have considerable potential in the propagation of broadband access. India looks forward to exploring possibilities of cooperation in R&D between India and other countries of the region, in the fields of ubiquitous mobile telecommunications, spectrum management techniques, digital audio-video broadcast and next generation terminal devices.

In this context, the need for shared research cannot be overstated. It would indeed be useful if a common R&D fund is created for the Asia Pacific region and utilized by identified centers of excellence in different countries so that research findings and developments can be shared freely on an Asia-Pacific telecommunity platform. Government and industry of the various countries can perhaps fund this research, along with contributions from the UN as well as multilateral funding agencies.

It may be recalled that one of the significant Millennium Development Goals is to make available, in cooperation with the private sector, the benefits of new technologies, especially in information and communications. The Asia Pacific region is home to a major segment of the world's population. Within this population, many areas are predominantly rural and governments thus face the challenge of removing poverty. Since communications is key to information, which in turn is vital for the removal of illiteracy, poverty and hunger, the need for sharing resources and strategies is obvious.

A project that could be of interest to the region is the setting up of an east-west information superhighway in order to have broadband connectivity from Iran/UAE to Vietnam via Pakistan, India, Bangladesh, Myanmar, Thailand, Malaysia and Cambodia. Apart from serving the region, this has the further advantage of acting as a standby route from Iran/UAE to Vietnam to the SEA-ME-WE 3 submarine cable and also to the forthcoming SEA-ME-WE-4 cable.

A proper regulatory framework would contribute significantly to the development of internet and broadband services. India has a very effective regulatory mechanism with adequate checks and balances. In the context of its shared commitment to improve broadband facilities in the region, it would be useful to share the Indian experience about regulatory mechanisms and study the course of further evolution.

Human resources are our major assets. These should be tuned to absorbing and managing the benefits of information and communication technologies. This calls for proper training of policymakers, managers, engineering professionals and content developers. India would be delighted to participate in this effort and offer its facilities as well as expertise in different domains, particularly in the field of planning and designing for rural communications. India would also be open to developing infrastructure facilities in other countries.

The internet knows no geographic boundaries. Even as the flow of information across the world is highly welcome, there are a number of issues that arise which call for intense cooperation between countries. As Eugene Ionesco said, “Dreams and anguish bring us together”.

Comment

N.R. Narayana Murthy
Chief Mentor, Infosys Technologies

India has set global benchmarks in the software industry. The past decade has witnessed major strides. Export revenues increased from $164 million in 1991 to around $10 billion in 2002—about 45% compounded annual growth rate (CAGR).

Today, India exports software services to over 100 countries. Employment has increased from around 30,000 in 1991 to over half a million today.

Globalization and the information revolution have raised customer expectations. They expect customer services at ever greater speeds and reduced costs. Consequently, corporations feel the need to increase productivity and efficiency by investing in information technology (IT).

According to the consulting firm, London Economics, investments in IT contributed 25% per annum to UK's output growth, and 47% to total labor productivity growth between 1992 and 2000. In the U.S., productivity growth rates nearly doubled during the late 1990s, from 1.4% (1972 to 1995) to 2.5% (1995 to 2000). The widespread adoption of IT was one of the most important factors contributing to this. In addition, McKinsey Global Institute (MGI) found that IT stimulated productivity by helping companies to innovate.

Thanks to intense pressures on performance, organizations have realized that IT is central to their strategy. GE, Capital One, Wal-Mart and HLL are examples of companies that have used IT to increase competitiveness.

Current trends in the global marketplace favor the continued growth of the IT industry, particularly in India. The dual pressures of a weak economy and the knowledgeable cusumer are forcing companies to revamp their business models. Thus, companies are increasingly focusing on their core businesses. They are looking outside their walls to outsource their non-core operations to value-for-money sources. This is an opportunity for India, which has come into the world's focus. According to a survey by Gartner, India was ranked by more than 70% of the large U.S. corporations surveyed as the primary country for supplying offshore IT services.

At the same time, there are also competitive forces in play. The Indian software industry faces stiff competition from East Asian countries such as China and the Philippines, and Eastern Europe. In addition, Indian IT majors are increasingly facing challenges posed by the multinational software and consulting firms that are establishing their offshore bases in India. According to a McKinsey survey, today, over 70% of the top 40 global IT services firms have their presence in India. These multinationals are focusing on the offshore outsourcing market.

In this context, there are several steps that India has to take to ensure the continued growth and vibrancy of this sector. Education is fundamental for a knowledge-based industry like software. It is predicted that approximately 1.1 million people will be needed by 2008. The supply of professionals, however, based on current trends, will fall short by over 200,000. Unfortunately, in India, total enrollment in higher education is only 6% of the relevant population (17-23 year olds). Our higher education institutions are unable to attract and retain high-quality faculty and research students. There is a lack of research focus. If the level of education in Indian colleges is to be improved, an impetus must be given to improving the level of R&D.

The country needs to ensure an adequate pipeline of English-speaking graduates. India has historically had an advantage over China and other East Asian countries in terms of its vast English-speaking population. However, India cannot become complacent. In Beijing alone, there are over a thousand language training centers. If India is to maintain its competitive advantage, the government must introduce spoken English courses in graduate and vocational colleges. It should also ensure that the English language is taught at all levels of education.

India needs to increase penetration in terms of PCs and communication lines. The high cost of ownership is a barrier against access to proliferation devices. The government has cut excise duties on hardware from 16% to 8%. This move increased PC sales. However, the cost of a PC is still too high for the masses.

Internet subscribers are expected to increase in number. This calls for additional investments in bandwidth. In addition, the availability of robust communication infrastructure is essential for Indian companies to effectively implement the offshore business model. As bandwidth requirements increase, greater investment in optical fiber networks and basic telecommunication networks is needed.

The software industry also requires good infrastructure and facilities. An open skies policy could allow more international flights out of IT hubs. While international airlines are keen to operate more flights to India, most of them consider negotiating commercial agreements with Air India and Indian Airlines cumbersome. Consequently, there is a huge demand-supply mismatch.

The open skies policy is especially important considering that the number of foreign travelers to India has increased dramatically over the past few years. In fact, business travelers accounted for about 60% of the total inflows in 2003. Unfortunately, between 1989 and 2000, the seat capacity on all international routes in India grew by a mere 40%. During the same period in China, it grew a whopping 485%!

Guaranteed and steady electricity supply is vital for the growth of any industry. At present, India ranks 75th, in terms of the quality of electricity supply. At conservative estimates, India's peak-load requirement will be 1.15 lakh MW at the end of the 10th Plan. This is another requirement that needs to be addressed.

India has more than 3 million kilometers of road network. Although this is the second largest in the world, it has increased by only seven times over the past 50 years, during which freight traffic had increased 67 times, and passenger traffic had increased 65 times! With traffic expected to grow by around 10% per year, the requirements for new roads would be 30,000 kilometers. It is obvious that money and effort need to be put into improving the road network.

As India moves towards being a knowledge-based economy, the protection of knowledge capital becomes essential. Software piracy rates are around 70%. This is substantially higher than the global average of 40%. In 2002 alone, India lost $340 million due to software piracy. A reduction from the current 70% level to 60% by 2006 will add $2 billion to India's economy, increase local industry revenues by around $1.6 billion, generate around 50,000 new high-tech jobs, and gain $92.4 million in tax revenues for the government.

Currently, exports are very dependent on the U.S. market which absorbs over 60% of total software exports. In order to de-risk and sustain growth, the industry should focus on other geographic markets. China represents an important export opportunity for the Indian software industry.

Given the current competitive scenario and falling margins for IT services, it is important that Indian companies move up the value chain by acquiring expertise in their clients' businesses. For global corporations, it is important to find a service provider that understands their business needs and IT goals. In this context, Indian service providers should evolve into 'business partners' with their clients, rather than just being 'service providers'. By doing so, they will be able to maintain India's position as the software destination of choice.

However, the digital divide is a major bottleneck to the growth and vibrancy of the industry. Growth cannot be sustained without including all sections of the population in the information revolution. India cannot have global competitiveness for the rich and illiteracy for the poor. Unfortunately, the country is increasingly being divided into people who do, and people who do not, have access to—and the capability to use—modern information technology.

About 70% of the Indian population lives in the villages, which are characterized by poor internet connectivity. Connectivity options to the rural areas can be improved by using wireless access. corDECT, an advanced, wireless access system developed by the TeNeT group of IIT Madras, Midas Communications and Analog Devices, is an instance of this. In addition, cyber cafes in the urban centers and village information kiosks in the rural areas will enhance the reach of IT.

India has a large population with great linguistic diversity. Local language content will make information and communication technology (ICT) more relevant and accessible to a broader cross-section of the population. Hence, the industry needs to develop applications that support local languages. In addition, voice applications that will let the masses interact with computers using the spoken language need to be developed.

IT literacy is critical to ensure that people can derive the appropriate benefits from the technology revolution. However, at a more fundamental level, providing basic education is the first step towards empowering the people. Today, only 65% of the population is literate, and only about 60% of India's children study up to class 5. In this regard, the government should focus on basic education. Further, private companies and NGOs should seek partnerships, in order to bring elementary computer literacy to people from rural India.

Besides making India competitive, ICT can help improve the lives of the masses. The anytime-anywhere and death-of-distance paradigms of technology enable better leveraging of scarce resources such as healthcare and education. In India, 51% of the population do not have access to essential drugs. Further, India has only 48 physicians per 100,000 population, compared to 279 for the U.S., and 162 for China.

ICT can help bring medical expertise to taluks and district headquarters. For instance, tele-medicine can link, via satellites, healthcare centers in remote locations to specialist hospitals at major towns/cities. Thus, it achieves connectivity between patients, at one remote end, and specialist doctors, for medical consultations and treatment. Narayana Hrudayalaya, for example, is a specialist cardiac care hospital in Bangalore which has pioneered the use of tele-medicine for extending cardiac care to remote areas of the country.

In a large developing country like India, there is a significant need for introducing transparency and efficiency in government functioning. Through e-governance, the government can provide the required infrastructure to effectively serve citizens' needs. By separating the delivery of services from decision making, the chances of corruption are reduced. Successes have already been made. In making the process more accessible and transparent, the Bhoomi project launched by the Karnataka government to digitize rural land revenue records has been a resounding success. Also, the internet has been used extensively as a communication channel for governments to reach out to their citizens. For instance, citizens can go online and monitor the progress of various government initiatives.

More than half of India's population is employed in agriculture. In this context, India has been a leader in the use of remote-sensing satellite information for locating irrigation projects. The internet has been used in some of the villages to ensure effective dissemination of agricultural commodity price information.

Distance education has tremendous potential to spread learning in India. E-learning is a cost-effective way of providing education at a distance. This is especially important, considering that around 85% of illiterate people in India are from the rural areas.

Today, the challenge for the Indian ICT sector is to enable the masses to leverage technology. At the same time, the industry needs to scale the global delivery model to meet increasing expectations from international customers. India can best achieve these objectives by investing in improving infrastructure and intellectual capital. In this way, the future of ICT in India can be ensured and the sector can continue to thrive and grow.

AGRICULTURE

Scenario

Dhruv M. Sawhney
Chairman and Managing Director, Triveni Engineering and Industries

This scenario is divided into four categories. First, I present a brief description on the potential of India's agriculture sector and a list of the problems facing private agri-business companies. Second, we look at the measures that the union and state governments need to take to facilitate greater investment in agriculture. Third, we examine what companies should do to capitalize on the potential. Finally, we consider how India's farmers can benefit from greater private corporate investment.

THE POTENTIAL AND THE PROBLEMS

On the demand side, India has a large domestic market for food and other agricultural commodities. More than one billion people have three meals a day and are dressed in clothes that are mostly made of cotton or silk. As India becomes richer, more people take to consuming milk, and meat or fish, fruits and vegetables. More Indian families consume processed and ready-to-eat foods.

India is also a medium-sized agricultural exporter, selling tea, fish, spices, and now rice and wheat to foreign countries.

On the supply side, there are four reasons for optimism:

1) India is blessed with fertile soils and many agro-climatic zones that can grow a range of produce. That is why it is the largest producer of milk, tea and cotton in the world, and second-largest producer of wheat and rice, and fruits and vegetables.
2) India's farmers are becoming more sophisticated and willing to use new technologies.
3) The government has built up a network of research laboratories and rural roads. Through a price support mechanism and together with the Food Corporation of India, the government has set up a way of

buying directly from farmers. While some of this infrastructure still remains to be modernized, the fact that it exists is reassuring.

4) Most importantly, Indian agribusiness companies are developing new models to reach out to farmers and consumers, providing new technologies, and investing more in modern supply chains and organized food retailing that sells more and more processed food.

However, Indian agriculture still suffers from many problems. Poor productivity of soil, falling water levels, expensive credit to farmers, a distorted market that does not send out the right price signals to farmers, intermediaries who increase the cost but do not add any value, government laws that stifle private investment, controlled prices, poor rural infrastructure, produce that do not meet international quality standards, inappropriate research and, worse still, a poor extension system, hamper the profit margins of farmers and companies. If Indian agriculture can survive despite these problems, if it is still able to feed all of India, and if these problems are eventually removed, India can dominate the world.

Five specific government-related problems confront agribusinesses. These are:

1) laws that force businesses to buy from monopoly markets at high prices, and not directly from farmers;
2) poor roads, and lack of access to power, warehouses and cold storages—all of which increase the cost of farm produce;
3) government price controls on many commodities, whether it is fertilizers or sugarcane, wheat or rice;
4) the different sets of laws in the 28 Indian states which sometimes make it difficult to move commodities from one state to another;
5) high taxes on processed foods, as compared to other developing countries, make these foods relatively more expensive for the majority of Indians.

INCREASING INVESTMENTS IN AGRICULTURE

Like their counterparts in the manufacturing and services sectors, agribusiness companies do not want government subsidies. Rather, they want an end to the system of government subsidies to farmers, which can result in higher support prices and distorted market prices. The government, in particular the state governments, should also remove the law that creates monopoly markets, which only drives up costs. This is the Agriculture Produce Marketing Commodity Act (APMC Act). Other laws that should similarly be removed include the law that makes it difficult to move commodities like sugarcane or milk from one state to the next.

The food processing industry would, however, like a new law to supersede the more than nine laws and ministries that currently regulate food—a unified food law.

The union government is trying to amend the APMC Act. A model act has been drafted and passed on to the state governments to aid the formulation of their state-specific legislation. In fact, 18 months ago, a group of ministers was brought together to come up with an integrated food law.

Basically, businesses would like the government to set Indian agriculture 'free'—free to buy at market-determined prices and free to buy from anywhere; free to sell at market-determined prices and in any location; and, free to make profits from agriculture, since without a profit, there will be no investment in agriculture.

The Confederation of Indian Industry (CII) believes that the union government has to play the important role of motivating state governments to carry out necessary reforms. Some of this was seen in the sugar package, where, in return for central funds, states could no longer set state-advised prices for sugarcane, which was often higher than the center's statutory minimum price.

At the same time, there should be uniform taxation in Indian agriculture, with lower rates for all items that go into agriculture and food processing.

In addition, the government should also help to create a viable crop insurance system. Today, while crop insurance exists, it does not entirely cover the risks of each farmer, and the premiums collected are too low.

THE ROLE OF BUSINESSES

Businesses have five important roles to play in Indian agriculture.

1) Businesses must ensure that farmers get the latest technologies, but at affordable prices. Indian farmers will soon have to compete with their counterparts in other countries as agricultural trade is liberalized. They need access to the right inputs, including the latest technologies. Indian agribusinesses have to improve on not just their research, but also their marketing skills, in order to reach even the small farmers. This not only applies to inputs, but also to other services like finance, soil testing, weather advice, price advice, etc.
2) They need to work with farmers to improve the quality of their produce so that it meets domestic and international standards. This requires that farmers be given information about what to grow, what inputs to use, and what prices to expect.
3) They should also invest in brand-building, value addition and exports, all of which build sustained demand and generate higher income for both farmers and businesses. This is especially true of exports. Indian businesses must take the lead in exporting higher quality produce to foreign markets, which in turn will have a positive effect on farmers. They would be encouraged to grow better produce. Domestic consumers will also slowly begin to demand higher standards.
4) They could work with government research institutions, banks, and other players in agriculture to improve the competitiveness of Indian agriculture. This would include strengthening the supply chain so that the costs of the final produce are competitive in world markets.
5) Businesses can help in linking farmers to markets, so that farmers grow only those commodities which fetch the highest prices in a free market. Today, in a distorted market, farmers' decisions are not necessarily the most economically rational. Once the government removes various restrictions, it will then be the responsibility of businesses to link farmers to markets by giving them information about prices (price discovery), by setting up alternative markets, by increasing the buying of those products that can be sold and by helping farmers to lower their cost and their risk.

FARMERS' BENEFITS

First, farmers have to accept the logic of liberalization, which is that prices can go up or down, depending on demand. If they are willing to adopt modern farm management practices, they can be as prosperous as their cousins elsewhere in the world.

However, to benefit further, farmers need to be organized so that they can demand more from governments and businesses: the right policies from government, appropriate and affordable inputs from businesses and the ability to sell their produce at the best price.

Indian agribusinesses realize that they cannot do well if Indian farmers do not prosper. Similarly, once farmers realize that companies are not out to exploit them, but want to give them the best possible support so that they can grow the highest-quality crops which can be sold at good prices, then farmers and companies will be able to work in true partnership.

Strengthening the partnership between the company and the farmer is important, because the earlier relationship between the farmer and the government is breaking down. Governments no longer have the money to subsidize inputs or even the final commodity. Despite political lobbying, most state governments will soon run out of funds to continue subsidies. As it is, subsidies in Indian agriculture are three times the public investment in agriculture. The private sector is the only other investor in agriculture, but for such investments to take off, both sides need to honor their responsibilities.

There is one more imperative for urgent internal reforms in agriculture, and that is the threat of international competition after the completion of WTO negotiations. If Indian agribusiness does not become more competitive through internal reform while it still has time in the next few years, then it will be too late to deal with more competitive foreign countries in a few years' time.

The CII believes that the Indian agribusiness can become more competitive, and that Indian farmers and businesses can do much more together than they had done in the past. If the government frees agriculture from many outdated controls, then everyone will benefit.

Comment

Gilbert Etienne
Professor Emeritus, University of Geneva

The preceding report presents a fine analysis of Indian agriculture—its wide potential and its weak points. It deals at length with agribusiness. My purpose is to add some comments on the basic problems of agriculture and the rural economy. Second, I would like to underline the conditions required for a big push to the rural economy that would result in deep social and economic implications, i.e. a faster decline of poverty, a situation more acute in villages than in cities; and, a faster growth of GDP under rising push and pull effects between industry and agriculture, and between consumption in rural and urban areas.

SLOWDOWN IN AGRICULTURAL GROWTH

Hydraulic Works

Minor works (tubewells, pumpsets) have seen an enormous expansion since the 1950s, stimulated by widespread rural electrification. Since the late 1970s, the supply of electricity has deteriorated at varying degrees due to poor O/M expenditures and the lack of investments at the national and state levels. 30% of electric supply is devoted to agriculture. Long power breakdowns or sheer lack of current severely affect crops.

Another matter of concern is, especially in northwest India, the excess of tubewells so that the recharge of ground water is in danger. There have been major irrigation works on the canals, barrages and dams. The maintenance of canals has been poor since the 1960s, so that only 30 to 40% of water entering the canals reaches the crops. Besides, there is a large and continuing gap between the potential created by new major works and the area actually irrigated (9 million ha in 2003) due to all kinds of delays, including lack of public funds and the persistent trend to start too many works at a time. Tanks in South India suffer from neglect, although this is partly compensated by pumpsets. Because of these shortcomings, irrigated areas are vulnerable to drought. But a good monsoon can compensate for some of the deficiencies of the irrigation systems. Finally, water-saving systems such as sprinklers and drips should be more encouraged than is presently the case. But while flood control and drainage have made some progress, a lot remains to be done, especially in the lower Ganges Basin.

Rainfed Areas

Rainfed areas cover about 60% of the cultivated land. In many places, one cannot expect widespread irrigation because of the lack of surface and ground water. However, watershed development contributes to growth, albeit not in a spectacular manner. Such works could no doubt expand but they are complex and take many years to complete.

Use of Inputs

From the beginning of the Green Revolution (GR) in the late 1960s, in India as it was in other Asian countries, the use of chemical fertilizers has suffered from the imbalance between nitrogen, phosphate and potash (NPK). This leads to soil deterioration.

Basic Research

The present lack of public money cannot be fully compensated by private research. The latter, in India and elsewhere, tends to focus 'almost exclusively on highly commercial crops' while financial support for public sector institutions is stagnating if not falling (IFPRI Forum, 2020 Vision, Washington DC, March 2004).

Renewal of Seeds

Seeds of the GR must be renewed every four to five years (except hybrids, for which seeds are renewed every year), or the yields will decline. This process is not working well.

Pest Control

There are frequent complaints of inappropriate use of pesticides which can result in polluting the air and affecting yields.

Adulteration of Inputs

There are frequent complaints from farmers on the adulteration of chemical fertilizers and pesticides.

Extension Services

Agriculture is becoming increasingly sophisticated. However, extension services, instead of improving, are deteriorating or have stagnated.

Rural Infrastructure

The development of electricity and rural roads had been, once upon a time, instrumental for growth. Today, they have become major stumbling blocks to further progress.

Poor maintenance of roads has led to a growing deterioration of roads that were built in the 1960s through 1980s. This severely affects the transportation of goods and the use of motor vehicles. The costs of bad roads, delays, traffic jams and damage to vehicles run into billions of dollars every year. Besides, a number of villages still remain without all-weather roads and electricity.

Post-harvest Technologies

There is enormous room for improvement in agribusiness, local demand and exports. More efficient rice mills and better storage of cereals would improve the supply of food grains and prevent big losses. Cold-storage houses play a key role in the promotion of potatoes, vegetables, fruit, milk, meat, fish and flowers.

At present, their development is far from satisfactory. Coupled with poor transportation conditions, losses can come up to 30% for fruit and vegetables, and 60% for cabbage and tomatoes.

DIVERSIFICATION OF THE RURAL ECONOMY

Certain positive changes have partly compensated for the overall slowdown in agricultural growth. Diversification in the sector has been more active in the area of animal husbandry and the increased cultivation of milk, poultry, fruits, vegetables, fish ponds and aquaculture, and even flowers.

These high-value items contribute to growth and also have an important social value: the creation of more job opportunities for agricultural workers and small-plot owners.

Other areas that require improvement and that are important to the growth of the agriculture sector include the maintenance of brick factories and the replacement of mud walls by pukka houses, the progress of petty and organized trade, and the development of workshops and small factories. These activities would lead to a global process of rural development which would stimulate growth and create more employment, in and outside the agriculture sector. This is confirmed by agricultural wages in Green Revolution districts which are usually double of what is paid in slow-moving districts. There would also be greater job opportunities.

On the whole, plantations (tea, coffee, rubber) have recorded better results than other agricultural sectors, but they employ only a small number of workers and are confined to only a few areas.

INDIA'S RURAL AREAS

While the global process of rural development is still going on in spite of the above shortcomings, one could divide India's rural areas into three broad categories:

- The Green Revolution districts in the north western and the south eastern irrigated deltas of Andhra and Tamil Nadu. The yields of wheat and/or clean rice amount to 3,000–4,000 kg/ha per crop. An additional 1,000 kg per crop is possible provided the whole system—water supply, fertilizers, pesticides—operates as it does in advanced countries, a task not easy to reach under the present conditions. Besides, such progress would still not meet the demands of the rising population. Hence, accelerating the ongoing process of diversification in agriculture and in non-agricultural activities would be welcome.
- The Eastern plains, Bihar, Assam, Orissa, with the partial exception of West Bengal, have known for decades a sluggish growth and increasingly heavy population densities. This wide area is populated by a very large number of extremely poor people.

The Eastern Ganges basin has been, until the later part of the 19th century, one of the major granaries of India. It could become so again, thanks to excellent alluvial soils, considerable ground and surface water for irrigation and usually a fairly generous monsoon. 80 to 90% of the land area (West Bengal included) could be irrigated like the Green Revolution districts, instead of the 30-45% at present. Irrigated rice could thus enjoy, during the first stage, yields of 2,000-2,500 kg/ha instead of 1,000 or 1,500 when rainfed. In the dry season, one could reap 2,000 kg/ha of irrigated wheat. Such a breakthrough would considerably reduce acute poverty. Yields could gradually rise further and the diversification process would gather momentum.

- Peninsular India suffers from a limited and erratic rainfall in the western and central parts, resulting in low yields of coarse grain (500–800 kg/ha in a fairly good year). Although the yields of soybean and sunflower have expanded in the past 20 years, they are still not high. The northeast part of the peninsula enjoys a heavier monsoon, which gives yields of 700-1,000 kg/ha (clean rice). In these hilly terrains, there is low potential for irrigation.

Greater effort should be targeted at the areas with limited irrigation in order to boost horticulture and the cultivation of vegetables. Drip irrigation should be used, when possible. Recent experiences in Maharashtra are encouraging. In several major areas, massive progress made in watershed projects which have combined the fight against erosion and water conservation would bring yields of about 1,000 kg/ha of coarse grain and encourage the planting of fruit trees.

TOWARDS A BIG PUSH

M.S. Swaminathan, India's top agricultural scientist, referring to the 1994 Marrakesh agreement and to the Cancun conference in 2003, summarized the major constraints:

> "Between 1994 and 2003, we were busy finding fault with the WTO Agreement rather than paying attention to enhancing the productivity, quality, diversification, value addition and sustainability components of our agriculture... At the same time, we should realize that trade

liberalization without increased investments in agriculture and rural development will not help us to face the challenge of market efficiency." *The Hindu Survey of Indian Agriculture 2004*, p.8

One must add, however, that this lack of attention had started more than 10 years before Marrakesh. It remained so under the different governments that had come into power. The political manifestos of both the BJP and the Congress emphasised on more rapid development of the rural economy. This was repeated by the new prime minister, Manmohan Singh.

The first condition for success is the thorough commitment of the ruling elites, as exemplified in the introduction of the Green Revolution. At that time, Lal Bahadur Shastri, and then Indira Gandhi, aimed to cut India's dependency on USA for food aid and tried to make India self-sufficient in foodgrains. A superb minister of agriculture, C. Subramanyam and a small team of ICS /IAS officers of high caliber, conducted the operations with the very efficient assistance of the Ford and Rockefeller Foundations (which supplied the first high-yield varieties). It was later also supported by US AID and the World Bank.

Today, India does not need such assistance. It is up to the new government to show the necessary commitment. Will it be possible to curb the urban bias of a growing number of representatives of the elites? The gap between urban middle/upper castes and villagers is not new but it has widened in the past 20 years because of a lack of awareness about what happens away from cities. Should one at this stage remember how Mahatma Gandhi 'partly ruralized' the top leadership of the Congress in the 1920s? In terms of private corporations, not all of them have understood the importance of rural markets like Hindustan Lever has. Socio-political conditions in certain states, particularly Bihar, may also make a big push hard to implement.

With a total fiscal deficit amounting to 10% of GDP, the availability of public funds is an issue of concern. Would it be possible to cut subsidies for fertilizers, electricity, water charges etc? Can we cut back on anti-poverty programs which do not give significant results?

In other words, changes in the allocation of public money would favor productive tasks. Already in the 1990s, I had met landless agricultural laborers in Dalit asking for "bijli, sarak, pani" (electricity, roads and water) because they understood very well the social value of such investments, which are more important than dubious anti-poverty programs involving malpractices and corruption.

Strengthening district administration would also help, as it is a safer way than trying to widen the scope of Panchayati Raj. I have often observed the achievements of smart district magistrates who are really committed to development. In that perspective, it would be desirable to curb the trend observed in certain states to place promoted IAS officers (more vulnerable to local political pressures) as heads of districts, and instead directly recruit IAS officers for that position. The too-frequent transfers of IAS officers (after less than 10 months in Uttar Pradesh) are another obstacle to sustainable development.

Better cooperation and more mutual efforts between the government services and the private sector could reduce post-harvest losses and, boost agribusiness and food processing. Finally, we need to consider how to curb corruption and thefts, problems related to poor maintenance of infrastructure (bad roads, non-payment of bills, free or very cheap electricity), defects in anti-poverty programs, losses of cooperative credit societies and other activities. A number of civil servants, including many IAS officers, remain very decent, but their actions against malpractices are too often curtailed by politicians, and they end up in 'transfers'.

The vigorous commitment of the political leadership, availability of competent and talented civil servants and scientists to implement new policies, greater involvement of private enterprises, and strong response of farmers are all possible.

Comment

Yogesh C. Deveshwar
Chairman, ITC Ltd, India, and former President of the Confederation of Indian Industry, (2005-2006)

The entrepreneurial energies of the private sector need to be harnessed to bring about competitiveness in India's rural sector. As the economy globalizes, liberalization in the trading of agricultural products will pose formidable threats and exciting opportunities. Without competitiveness, rural employment is threatened. On the other hand, competitiveness can lay open the opportunities of remunerative world markets.

No Indian enterprise using agricultural raw materials can attain, in isolation, decisive international competitiveness. This competitiveness is inextricably intertwined with that of the farm sector and indeed, the entire value chain from the farmer to the consumer, both domestic and international. The corporate sector has a vested interest in contributing to, and securing the competitiveness of, the entire value chain of which it is a part.

One of the key objectives of second-generation reforms should be to fashion a climate in which the corporate sector can pursue its objective of creating shareholder value more readily by contributing to the prosperity of the Indian farmer. Traditionally, the Indian corporate sector has by and large viewed its contributions to the rural sector as part and parcel of its social responsibility, outside of its commercial objectives. Such contributions, therefore, tended to be either limited in scope or sustainability.

The imperative of creating competitiveness in the farm sector, and indeed, the entire value chain as a pre-condition for business success in a fast globalizing environment has prompted the corporate sector to seek solutions with urgency.

The two most commonly advocated solutions for improving farm economies are consolidation of land and contract farming. Both have evoked strong reactions from the farming community, particularly among small and marginal farmers, who are apprehensive about large-scale displacement of labor and fears of exploitation at the hands of more powerful corporate entities. This is one reason why there is political hesitation in gathering support for contract farming, even though contract farming is the quickest way to bring about efficiencies.

An alternative model that captures the advantages associated with contract farming, yet engages and distributes the resources of the corporate sector more equitably among farmers, would be more appropriate to the unique structure of Indian agriculture at this point in time and hence, better preferred. As the rural infrastructure in India matures, and the farming community develops a more pervasive sense of security borne out of prosperity, there will be a wider acceptability of ideas like land consolidation and contract farming.

Rapid developments in technology, particularly information technology, make such a model conceivable. The primary ingredients of the alternative model are:

- the use of information technology to deliver real-time information and customize knowledge to improve farmers' decision-making abilities, so that they align farm output to market demands, secure quality and productivity, and improve price discovery;
- the use of information technology to aggregate demand in the nature of a virtual producers' cooperative in order to access high quality farm inputs and knowledge at the lowest cost; and,
- the use of information technology to set up a direct marketing channel virtually linked to the mandi system for the purposes of price discovery (without wasteful intermediation) and multiple handling, in order to reduce transaction costs and make logistics efficient and cost-effective.

The corporate entity that invests in such an e-infrastructure and creates abiding value for the farmer in this manner would be rewarded in more ways than one—he would be known as a trustworthy supplier of goods, services and inputs, and as a buyer of cost-effective quality farm outputs to support competitiveness in the marketplace. This infrastructure can also be used for channeling services related to credit, insurance, health and education.

Such an approach is illustrative and can, with appropriate modifications, be applied to all facets of agriculture like floriculture, sericulture, horticulture, aqua farming, poultry farming and animal husbandry. International competitiveness can thus be engendered (wherever it is feasible) to create a structure where the corporate sector's need for creating shareholder value can be enmeshed with that of the farming community in a mutually supportive, interlocking and interdependent partnership.

Utopian as it might appear at first sight, this model is not merely a fancy academic exercise. My company has demonstrated the feasibility of this model through its click and mortar initiative titled 'e-Choupal'. It is a matter of pride for me to share with you that this initiative has already become one of rural India's largest internet-based interventions, reaching out to some quarter million farmers in two thousand villages through 460 choupals in the states of Madhya Pradesh, Karnataka and Andhra Pradesh. The customization of the content to local requirements and in the local language has made it user-friendly for the farmer. This model has met with enthusiastic response from farmers, and has thus led us to plan for the extension of this initiative to another eleven states. This pioneering initiative is a manifestation of my company's commitment and is based on the understanding that Indian agri-based exports would sustainably create value only if the entire value chain from farmer to consumer is internationally competitive.

The growing competitiveness of Indian agriculture induced through such a market-led business model can trigger a virtuous cycle of higher productivity, higher incomes, enlarged capacity for farmer risk management, higher order of investments, and higher quality. On the other hand, growth in rural incomes would also unleash the latent demand potential for industrial goods so necessary to launch the economy into a higher growth trajectory.

I may have overstated my case if I have given the impression that such an endeavor is a walk in the park. There are challenges primarily in the form of infrastructural inadequacies, including power supply, telecommunications connectivity and bandwidth, apart from the challenge of imparting skills to first-time internet users in remote areas of rural India.

The benefits of rural initiatives tend to be back-ended, thereby stretching corporate resources. One cannot expect everyone to be fired by passion alone. In order to mobilize wider participation by the private sector in a similar pursuit, governments, the center and state can play a catalytic role by crafting a nurturing policy framework. Incentives to encourage investments in this sector could be confined to an initial period of say three to five years, until the rewards of the virtuous cycle kick in.

Another example of private sector involvement can be in the area of the wood-based industry. Biotechnology-based farm forestry programs would bring into productive use vast tracts of degraded private land, create the biomass to restore ecosystems, provide a sustainable source of productive employment among the weakest sections of the rural population, and secure a competitive source of wood-based raw material. Here again, my company together with select NGOs, has embarked upon a social farm forestry program that creates a mutually beneficial virtuous economic cycle with the marginal farmers in rural Andhra Pradesh. We have to extend our endeavors to transform India's rural sector.

INFRASTRUCTURE

Scenario

Robert Greenhill
former Chief Executive Officer, Bombardier International

The liberalization of the Indian economy has brought home the realization that India needs a more efficient transport system in order to be globally competitive. India's transport network is extensive, but its overall performance—especially surface transport—is poor.

Although the initial numbers seem impressive, the infrastructure is too old or too small to be internationally competitive. Economic losses from congestion and poor roads are estimated to be as high as Rs200-300 billion (US$4.3–$6.5 billion) a year.

Within India, constraints on infrastructure capacity are widely claimed as the main reason for the poor services. But the problem is more complicated than that. A number of operational weaknesses not only reduces service quality, but also exacerbates capacity shortages—especially in operations dominated by the public sector where there is little competition.

Transportation infrastructure in India is improving. The question is whether the infrastructure is improving quickly enough, given India's mounting requirements to move people and services, and given ongoing improvements in other countries.

Infrastructure improvement is in a race against time in India, and India's accelerated economic growth is at stake.

DEMAND GROWTH IN TRANSPORT SERVICES

Demand growth for transportation services appears to be accelerating. In India, the demand elasticity of transport services over economic growth ranges from 1.2 to 1.4. What this means is that to reach 8% growth for a sustained period of time, transportation capacity must increase by 10-12% per year.

Many long-term trends are evident:

- Road transport is expected to increase its modal share due to the development of the Golden Quadrilateral.
- The decline in the market share of railways is going to continue until reforms to railways are implemented and the system becomes more commercially-oriented.
- Growth in international trade and investment will increase demand for international air and ocean transport, multimodal transport as well as high quality, high frequency international and domestic air services.
- Rapid urbanization and motorization will increase pressure on already congested cities, thereby creating a need for modern and affordable urban transport solutions.

SUPPLY-SIDE PROBLEMS

Despite improvements in some areas such as the roads in the Golden Quadrilateral, supply has not kept pace with the mounting demand. This is due to five major problems which affect every transportation sector, although some more than others.

1) Lack of agreement on transportation's primary role as supporting sustained economic growth
2) Unclear and fragmented responsibilities for setting policy, managing critical transportation infrastructure, running operations and overseeing results
3) Chronic lack of investment capital in high-quality transportation infrastructure
4) Weak management of assets and less-than-optimal allocation of scarce resources
5) Absence of effective systems which would allow transport users to make transport agencies account for their performance

ASSESSMENT OF REFORMS

In the last decade, the pace of reforms in the sub-sectors of the transportation infrastructure had varied. This is shown in the table (facing page).

Sector Policy	Roads	Railways	Ports	Urban	Aviation Transport
Private sector	5	1	4	3	3
FDI	5	1	5	4	3
Independent regulation	3	1	4	2	1
Legal reforms	5	1	3	3	2
Higher budgetary allocation	5	2	5	3	5
Liberal equipment imports	5	2	5	4	5
Public-private sector partnerships	5	2	4	3	1
Total	33	10	30	22	20

(Note: A value of 5 denotes positive developments while 1 denotes insignificant action.)

There are some encouraging recent examples of policy innovations:

- Highways: Launch of the National Highway Development Project (NHDP) and creation of NHAI, CRF and RDCs to address implementation and financing issues
- Railways: Some rationalization of tariff structures and reduction of cross-subsidy to passenger fares; creation of Container Corporation of India (CONCOR) and the launch of the Golden Quadrilateral project
- Ports: Phased corporatization of major ports and opening up to private sector and FDI with fiscal incentives; the attempt to keep regulation separate from other administrative issues by creating Tariff Authority for Major Ports (TAMP); development of minor ports; recent announcement to launch a 'Golden Sea Chain' project which will bring focus and accelerate reforms
- Urban Transport: Fiscal and administrative decentralization to local bodies and states through constitutional amendment; implementation of capital-intensive metro projects in Delhi through SPV-kind structure; pollution control through application of better technology and use of environment-friendly fuels in public transport systems
- Aviation: Introduction of competition on the domestic front by allowing entry of private sector airlines, leading to improvements to capacity and quality; putting airport privatization on track through constitutional amendment; allowing competition on international routes

Experts interviewed were satisfied with the government's performance on the roads and ports sector but were concerned over the situation with railways. They expressed an urgent need to press forth on improving urban transport infrastructure.

Experts believe that while the problem of poverty can be somewhat eased by building roads, the situation will nonetheless worsen if no concrete plan is drawn and implemented on improving urban transportation and the railway system.

VISION FOR THE FUTURE

If India is to meet its ambitious growth target of 8% in GDP over the period of the 10th Plan, then the capacity of its transportation system has to grow by 10-12% per year—that is an increase of 150-200% in the next 10 years. Because many of the infrastructure projects have long gestation periods of 5-10 years, policy and investment decisions taken now will determine the limits to India's growth a decade from today.

Over a 10-year period, India should achieve two goals in order to reach global standards in transportation infrastructure:

1) Capacity enhancement and more competitive operations in existing infrastructure through policy and operational improvements
2) Creation of better and more modern infrastructure through greater investments

India's own experience and international best practices point to a few critical elements for success:

- Clear public policy responsibility—one government body with authority to act in a comprehensive manner (e.g. a single highway policy authority)
- Building institutional capacity (human resources and equipment) in Indian government agencies to develop, implement and oversee world-class transportation and infrastructure policies, to handle new technology to react to emerging issues (environment etc.)
- A clear policy roadmap coupled with resolution of outstanding legal and regulatory constraints to improve access to private finance

- Splitting-up of policy, implementation, and enterprise management
- Unbundling of transportation systems to allow maximum competition where appropriate (for example, in the rail system, allow vendors to compete to operate canteens and other support services)
- Overcoming social concerns of restructuring by building a social safety net to protect retrenched labor
- Making social policy elements distinct and market-oriented, instead of using them as a cash cow (e.g. in aviation) or embedding social programs within them (e.g. subsidization of passenger rail travel and airline category III route service requirements)
- Self-financing on the 'user-pays' principle is often the best. Capture a share of associated value creation (e.g. the increase of property values around a new airport) to help cover costs. While subsidies may be required on certain projects, e.g. urban mass transit, the support should be carefully calibrated against international benchmarks.
- Transparency to ensure that the right investments are made, with the lowest cost and most efficient operations. It is very tempting for major infrastructure projects to fall prey to parochial interests—rent-seeking bureaucrats, local biases, political factors and regional favoritism. A well-structured delineation of responsibilities and transparent processes will help mitigate this danger.

Concrete opportunities for improvement abound in the transportation sector.

- Roads: Continue with recent developments and extend to major state highways and rural roads; price and manage traffic carefully to avoid congestion; ensure an appropriate engineering technology for feeder roads
- Rail: Make policy changes (e.g. reduce number of stops for slow-moving trains), operational improvements, and signal to investments to increase the effective capacity of existing lines; unbundle operations (strip-out non-core businesses; provide choice and competition where appropriate in core businesses; accelerate the development of state-of-the-art multimodal container services

- Ports: Maintain the momentum; avoid unnecessary duplication and make clear-headed assessments on how best to use port facilities in the surrounding region; determine when best to compete, when best to leverage other country's facilities (e.g. Colombo's deep-water port); de-bottleneck the custom procedures to reduce holding time and documentation
- Urban centers: Get the act together quickly; shift transport responsibilities to state and local governments and facilitate the process of building financial and institutional capacity; for each major city, develop a comprehensive transportation plan that is integrated with a land use plan; take steps to improve traffic management and discourage use of personal transport
- Aviation: Allow full competition on all routes (recently proposed); eliminate the fuel tax—a most regressive tax; rationalize airport charges; over time, eliminate category III restrictions and provide subsidies for essential air services where required (with costs shared by national/state/local authorities); improve the quality of and access to airports—privatize or municipalize; develop a robust traffic management system that addresses relevant technical issues and meets strategic objectives, so that rising demand for air traffic is supported by a safe, secure and efficient mechanism

If key players show the required vision and courage, there will be multi-billion-dollar investment opportunities for Indian businesses to become world-class builders and managers of transportation infrastructure. If the reform process is expedited, the Indian transport infrastructure is going to see a lot of action in the next 10 years. A massive requirement for national and international capital will create opportunities for financial institutions, foreign investors and infrastructure players, and stimulate various industries such as cement, steel, equipment, consultancy and engineering.

The quantum of investments expected in the next decade is:

- Roads: US$40 billion
- Ports: US$20 billion
- Railways: US$15 billion
- Urban transport: US$5 billion
- Aviation: US$7 billion

While these potential opportunities do exist, there are many implications for all stakeholders, including the government, before these opportunities can materialize.

- Government: The government needs to come up with clear and consistent policy guidelines to ensure long-term and well-coordinated decisions. To accelerate development, the government needs to strike a balance between the need for immediate action, and the need for public and private sector learning and capacity-building. The government needs to pay specific attention to contract management and regulation in order to create a level playing field with appropriate levels of risk-sharing.
- Multilateral Agencies: Institutions like the WB and ADB have a key role to play. They must encourage the development of new revenue streams such as direct-user charges. Further, their support must be focused on strengthening institutions and promoting a clear distribution of roles between the public and private sectors, rather than just providing pure budget finance for projects.
- Industry: Industry will need to lobby to ensure that the momentum gained is not lost and that the government creates an environment conducive to implementing global best practices, adapted to Indian conditions. Industry should promote international partnerships, so that Indian companies can leverage international experience and foreign companies can leverage the local knowledge of Indian companies.

Lastly, India provides a unique opportunity because of its huge size and population. Successfully implementing transportation infrastructure reforms could create a whole new category of world-class Indian businesses. In transportation infrastructure, the appropriate investments in R&D, specialized equipment, key skills and human resources to meet India's own needs will allow many Indian companies to reach world-class levels of critical mass and competence. Industry can then leverage these world-class, low-cost solutions and introduce them to other world markets. For example:

- Airline maintenance and overhaul is an area where India could develop a major international business, leveraging its low labor costs and world-class engineering capabilities to service aircrafts.

- A privatized and competitive railcar-manufacturing sector should provide better cost and quality to India's railways as well as encourage the exporting of locally-made products to the world markets.
- There are many transportation-related service businesses—architecture, civil engineering and information systems—for which India could develop world-class skilled labor at low cost.

India could develop a real competitive advantage over major markets in the Asian-Pacific, African and Latin American regions which have similar transportation infrastructure requirements.

In conclusion, dealing with India's transportation infrastructure will not only provide India's existing companies with the efficient transportation system they need in order to take on the world, it would create a whole new set of world-class Indian players in the transportation sector.

Comment

Rakesh Mohan
Deputy Governor, Reserve Bank of India

Infrastructure investment used to be a staid, regular, uninteresting activity that the public sector was involved in and was taken for granted by most of the population. The kind of active discussion, experimentation and innovation that has taken place over the past decade is unprecedented in the area of infrastructure in India, and in the rest of the world. It is now time for consolidation and actual implementation. It is inescapable that if India is to achieve the kind of economic growth rates that have now become a matter of common aspiration, infrastructure must become even more of a priority than it has ever been.

That the public sector financing constraint is an objective reality has been documented in this book. The lesson is twofold. First, all constraints to private sector investment must be loosened so that some compensation can be made to the lower than desirable level of public investment. Second, there is no escape from raising the levels of infrastructure investment of the public sector since some infrastructure services are really public goods, whereas others exhibit partial public good characteristics. However, it will not be feasible to restore public sector infrastructure investment levels to appropriate levels without fiscal improvements, particularly through revenue increases in both tax and non-tax areas.

RURAL INFRASTRUCTURE

There has been a significant slowdown in agricultural growth over the past five years. Even prior to this period, growth trends had been in the region of 3% annual growth, although it had accelerated to 4.5-5.0% during the early to mid-1990s. If India is to approach annual growth of 7-8% over the next 5-10 years, agriculture cannot merely grow at rates of 2-3% annually.

In the past, growth in agriculture had been equated with growth in the production of foodgrains. It is now clear that, with rising incomes all round, the average Indian diet in both rural and urban areas is becoming increasingly diversified.

Consequently, expenditure on foodgrains as a proportion of total household food expenditure is falling. Growth in domestic demand for foodgrains is, therefore, unlikely to sustain growth in production greater than what has been achieved in the past. Higher agricultural growth will now have to come from a much more diversified agriculture sector as has been the experience in other fast-growing Asian countries.

Agricultural diversification and accelerated agricultural growth will be difficult to achieve without much greater investment in rural infrastructure such as roads, storage facilities, telecommunications, power, and the like. Diversified agriculture will need much more complex commercial linkages between the farm and market. Thus, rural infrastructure investment will yield high economic returns, but it is difficult to develop any methodology to yield adequate financial returns. States such as Punjab, Haryana, Kerala, Tamil Nadu and Goa that invested in rural roads relatively early have demonstrated how essential it is to do so.

A key challenge for India in the coming years will be the investment in and financing of rural infrastructure. Given the difficult fiscal situation, innovation will have to be the order of the day. New approaches to public-private partnerships, participation of local governments, and funds sourced from dedicated levies such as the fuel cess will all have to be explored. It will also have to be understood politically that a continuation of tariff policies such as the low rural electricity tariffs will not contribute to the rapid development of rural infrastructure.

REGULATION

Increases in private sector investments can take place on both the exclusive and partnership bases. In sectors such as telecommunications, where service users can pay user charges at economic levels, there is no constraint, in principle, on exclusive private sector investment. The main area of policy concern in such sectors is the removal of regulatory risk. The rapid technological change that characterized telecommunications over the past decade gave rise to unavoidable regulatory changes, which often trailed technology. New kinds of services became possible, and falling equipment prices often gave new entrants an advantage over incumbents, giving rise to disputes over tariff issues.

This is similar to the case of the power sector, where information technology has made possible consumer choice and competition where none was thought feasible earlier. Here also, regulators have had to cope with new forms of organizational frameworks that require new kinds of regulatory intervention. These kinds of problems are intrinsic to sectors where rapid technical change takes place.

There are other kinds of regulatory risks that can indeed be removed. These relate to regulatory predictability and transparency. The principles of regulation must be thought out properly, articulated transparently and reasoned well. They must be technically sound so that they can be understood and accepted by market participants. If this is done, abrupt and ad hoc changes will automatically be avoided and private investment will flow.

However, the various regulatory authorities in India are still very new and can still be characterized as being on a steep learning curve. They have been handicapped by the lack of technical expertise at both the staff and management levels. Thus, many of their operations can be characterized as 'learning by doing'.

Staffing at the management level has typically been through the re-employment of retired civil servants; and at the staff level, through temporary secondments of civil servants from government departments. The authorities have exhibited a marked reluctance to hire from the market, both at the management and staff levels. Regulatory authorities in other countries typically have a better mix of staff that includes technical experts hired from the market, along with a sprinkling of civil servants.

With the imposition of public sector compensation structures, it is difficult to attract appropriate expertise at any level. Thus, a key requirement is that regulatory authorities must be financially and administratively autonomous. The remuneration of technical staff must be market-related and made transparent for accountability. Ultimately, they are responsible for their actions before the government and parliament, hence, accountability must be built into the governance structure of the regulatory organization.

Some regulatory risk arises from government or political interference in the work of the regulator, though it would be naïve to argue that the regulator must be completely immune to political and government pressures. The regulator is ultimately responsible to the government and parliament.

This problem of interference can be reduced by the articulation of conditions and if the government can give directions to the regulator in a transparent manner. As has been the case in Sri Lanka, for example, where government direction results in revenue loss to the operators, the government must have a responsibility to provide equivalent budgetary funds for that loss.

Tariffs are both the most contentious of issues that regulators handle, and also the raison d'etre for their formation. It is often with the objective of removing the tariff-setting processes from political pressures that regulators are established. Hence, it is doubly important for the government to develop procedures and conventions that allow regulators to function independently in tariff-setting, as well as to approach the achievement of a bipartisan consensus on tariff issues. This would involve wide public education and discussion on principles of pricing utilities. It is only if there is a better understanding of these issues, and of the necessity of economic pricing, that there can be any hope of regulators being allowed to do rational economic pricing.

More independence, financial autonomy, and better technical expertise of the regulatory authorities will do much to remove avoidable regulatory risk. The distancing of government from tariff decisions will reduce the inevitable special interest lobbying that often results in dysfunctional outcomes. Finally, transparency in the appointments process would greatly contribute to the independence and credibility of regulators.

FINANCING

The second issue related to private sector investment in infrastructure is the availability of adequate and structured financing. Each infrastructure sector has its own characteristics and financing mechanisms need to correspond to these characteristics. For example, once a power station or toll road is built, and tariffs are set in a transparent and predictable manner, cash flows will be fairly regular and predictable. They can then be securitized easily.

Having said that, it is widely noted, however, that the pre-operation risk is extremely high. Hence, risk mitigation and credit enhancement are necessary to attract resources at reasonable cost. Market instruments need to be designed to meet these requirements, along with specific government interventions, where necessary, in order to mitigate pre-operative risk.

The 1990s witnessed a great degree of innovation in structured finance all across the world. The huge expansion of cross-border flows of capital aided this explosion of innovation. It was also the period during which the former socialist economies made their transition towards the market system. All of them had large backlogs of infrastructure investment that had to be financed. Similarly, China, Indonesia and other fast growing East Asian countries exhibited great demand for infrastructure finance.

The exuberance of international capital flows, particularly towards developing countries, has dampened during this decade and hence needs some revival. As already noted, the initial expectations of return on equity were perhaps excessive, and particularly unsuited to infrastructure investment. Thus, the issue of international arrangements for cross-border flows of finances for infrastructure investment needs to be revisited.

International financial institutions can look more carefully from the point of view of both the investors and recipients. In some cases, large investments have been made for the privatization of existing utilities, particularly in Latin America. In other cases, green field investments have also been made in areas such as telecommunications, power and roads. Serious problems have arisen for investors where large changes have taken place in currency adjustments, a situation characteristic of the 1990s. Equity investors consequently suffered loss of returns whereas, in the case of debt, recipient countries encountered debt-servicing problems.

These issues need to be given due attention in the discussions related to the new financial architecture. Mechanisms have to be evolved to provide some protection to both potential investors and recipients so that large financial flows for infrastructure investments can be rekindled. Mechanisms could be devised for the credit enhancement of borrowers. Similarly, it should be possible to find ways and means for providing a floor for return to investment below which some form of investment insurance kicks in. The floor should clearly be below the level of market return to minimize moral hazards.

Various developments have taken place in the recent past that should make it easier for resources to be intermediated towards infrastructure projects. The government securities market has developed well and hence, debt market benchmarks are now available. It is now a rather liquid market and government securities can also be traded in the stock exchanges. The technological infrastructure for the debt market is thus in place in the stock exchanges. Interest rate derivatives are about to be introduced to aid risk management. An act enabling securitization of receivables on a widespread basis was passed recently. The same act has also strengthened creditor rights.

The Infrastructure Development Finance Company (IDFC) was founded in 1997 as a joint venture between the government of India, the Reserve Bank of India, domestic financial institutions, and foreign investors like the Asian Development Bank (ADB) and the International Finance Corporation (IFC), among others. Thus, institutional financing is also available for infrastructure.

In fact, credit disbursed from the banking system for infrastructure has increased from 1% of overall non-food credit in March 1998 to 3% at end-March 2003. IDFC itself has disbursed Rs28.5 billion as at March 2002. Thus, credit is widely available for viable infrastructure projects.

The equity market has generally been dormant since the mid-1990s. Hence, raising private equity has not been easy, particularly with the decline of the Unit Trust of India (UTI). Accordingly, a new initiative, the India Development Fund, has been put in place to help private sector promoters raise equity. It is expected that this fund will soon amount to Rs10 billion.

Furthermore, private sector insurance companies have begun operations and the entry of independent pension funds has now been announced. With these developments, a greater variety and volume of institutional investors are now available to support both direct and indirect investments in infrastructure. Thus, institutional investors such as banks, insurance companies, pension funds and the like can increasingly create specialized vehicles to channel equity funds into infrastructure projects, where risk capital is otherwise scarce. International infrastructure funds were the rage in the 1990s. They need to be replicated domestically in India now, but perhaps with a greater degree of realism in terms of expected returns. If such infrastructure equity funds succeed, they can also operate as credit enhancement vehicles, bringing other equity investors to the market in their wake.

A major development that has taken place in recent years is the significant reduction in inflation on a sustained basis, both internationally and in India. It was during the days of 7-10% annual inflation that equity investors, particularly international investors, expected 20-25% returns on risk capital. With inflationary expectations coming down to 3-5%, there should be a corresponding reduction in both costs of debt and equity. This should also make formerly unviable projects viable, and amenable to commercial investment. The consequent reduction in user charges necessary for viability would also come down, leading to greater acceptability.

India also needs to learn the different financing techniques employed in developed countries—essentially, private financing of public infrastructure and private-public partnerships. Two patent examples come to mind.

In the United States, municipal bonds, having been made tax-free by the federal government, enable local governments to tap the large U.S. capital market to finance local urban and other infrastructure. Because of the tax-free status (in recognition of the element of public good in providing urban infrastructure), the local governments could raise finances at lower cost, thus keeping user charges at affordable levels and municipal taxes at acceptable rates. The institution of municipal bonds provides internalized incentives for local authorities to be fiscally prudent—defaults on municipal bond servicing can cause great hardship.

The *pfandbrief* system in Germany is another example of effective private financing of public infrastructure. In this case, large mortgage banks pool local authority debt into '*pfandbriefs*', a process that enhances the credit of entities that may not otherwise be creditworthy. Underlying this system is a complex array of government guarantees. In spite of hyperinflation and two world wars, *pfandbriefs* have succeeded in keeping up credit quality for more than a hundred years.

In India as well as other developing countries, thought needs to be given to how such innovative systems can be derived to generate greater private financing of infrastructure.

In sum, there continues to be great opportunities for devising viable financing systems for funding infrastructure in both the public and private sectors. Today, much information is available on different techniques; technology makes possible financing systems not available earlier; and cross-border flows can again be rekindled. The fall in inflation and interest rates should also make hitherto unviable projects financially viable.

MANAGEMENT IN THE PUBLIC SECTOR

Even if all constraints are removed for private sector investments, the public sector would still have a very significant presence in infrastructure, both in existing entities as well as in new investments. Most roads, except for toll roads, will necessarily remain within the domain of the public sector, as will sewerage systems, public lighting and other similar components of urban infrastructure. Having large public good elements embedded in them, water supply systems, particularly distribution systems, are natural monopolies. Water generation, purification, treatment, etc. can indeed be privatized but the rest of the system will either remain in the hands of the public sector or be heavily regulated.

Similarly, for the railways, it is difficult to privatize the common carrier, i.e. the track, whereas the operation of trains and maintenance, etc. can potentially be privatized. Activities such as operation of terminals, traffic handling and, airline operations and shipping are typically the domain of the private sector, but port or airport ownership typically fall within the activities of the public sector. Thus, public investment in infrastructure will remain essential for an indefinite period of time, and will be crucial for a good part of its operations.

This must be understood and appreciated better. A much greater focus, than is the case at present, must be placed on public sector management. The public sector that continues to exist in infrastructure must be commercially-oriented and must have the best of management skills, since infrastructure systems are typically large systems. There is a great need for instilling excellence in public management systems. Capabilities need to be built up to bring in modern management systems. The system must attract the best managers.

As happens in many systems, the public sector and governmental management systems in India have become ossified with excessive rigidities and careerism built in. Entry into these systems is essentially at the basic level, with little or no mobility of personnel at higher levels. There is little infusion of new blood at higher levels, except at the board level, and excessive in-breeding and inward-looking attitudes have become the norm. Increasingly though, it has become clear that the system of promotion by seniority is not conducive to commercial operations.

What is needed is a system of induction of outside expertise at all levels in an organized framework. Labor mobility is hampered by the rigidities in the social security system where pensions and other similar benefits are not portable.

Great change in management systems has taken place in India and around the world. Public sector management, be it in public sector enterprises or central, state or municipal governments, needs to be modernized to take on the new challenges. Public sector systems are typically large systems and therefore, intrinsically more challenging. Young people of high caliber need to be attracted to these activities in much the same way as the best and most dynamic corporations attract the best talent to their portals.

In the current system in India, which now has a mix of public and private companies in the same sector, great inequalities in compensation have appeared between people performing similar functions. This issue needs to be tackled head-on and an acceptable methodology found to address it.

A major issue in public sector management is the tenure of chief executives. With the Indian Railways, for example, the chief executive seldom has a tenure of more than a year. With such a short tenure, he cannot be expected to have a medium-term vision, let alone a long-term one of bringing any change into the system. Even if he did, he certainly would have no chance of implementing it. However, flying in the face of this, experience in India has shown that in cases where there has been stability of leadership, enterprises have performed relatively well.

There is a great need, therefore, for new thinking on public sector management. Whereas privatization must be pursued with vigor, it is equally important to instil pride and excellence in public sector management.

PUBLIC-PRIVATE PARTNERSHIPS

Given that most infrastructure sectors exhibit some public good characteristics, investment can be maximized through public-private partnerships. If the achievable returns on an infrastructure activity through the levy of user charges is, say, 70% of market returns, a public subsidy of 30% would elicit market-based private investment, and the enterprise can then run on a commercial basis.

One example of such an activity has already been given in the case of toll roads. Another example could be that of urban water supply, where some water has to be given free for the less well-off through public standposts. Yet another example could be unremunerative railway lines that are deemed necessary for other objectives.

Such partnerships are, however, not easy to forge in a democratic parliamentary framework—questions inevitably arise on award of concessions and contracts. Hence, a great deal of work needs to be done to devise methodologies for the development of public-private partnerships. This also requires excellence in public sector management.

Comment

Ajit Gulabchand
Chairman and Managing Director, Hindustan Construction

No one will question the World Economic Forum's assertion that transport infrastructure is a critical driver of growth, distribution and global competitiveness, nor that it is one of the 10 pillars for sustained growth of the economy. The criticality of an efficient and high-quality transport infrastructure to competitiveness cannot be overstated. India's transport infrastructure, in absolute terms, appears deceptively gargantuan. But what is equally true is that poor quality and service make it fall miserably short in qualitative terms and global standards. The annual loss due to inadequate and inefficient transportation is $4-6 billion, which accounts for almost 1% of India's GDP. This imposes a burden on the economy and erodes competitiveness.

India's freight logistics is among the worst in the world. Even when compared with a similarly large country like China, it is 2.5 times slower. Transport infrastructure exists in significant quantum but quality transportation is non-existent. Investment lags are plentiful. India has to catch up on time, quality, costs and systems in order to achieve globally comparable levels.

The task of catching up on the backlog, of accelerating the expansion and of upgrading roads is Herculean, but vital for sustained growth and for gaining parity with major competitors like China. It is heartening to know that the government has taken the challenge in the right earnest spirit.

Given the enormous funds required, it is absolutely essential that every dollar is spent efficiently and on time. Indian project management is rife with delays and the costs of these delays are very high. It is therefore important that planning is meticulous and the execution of road projects is efficient. Projects need to be finely detailed so that unexpected costs are minimal. Unfortunately, this is not the case. The process of planning and implementation of road-building must be audited.

There are several policies which unnecessarily inflate costs and for which the government pays the price and all are losers. For example, pre-qualification norms often insist on ownership of modern equipment. When a project is broken into packages, each contractor has to comply with the requirements.

In the case of the Mumbai Pune Expressway, for example, all the contractors had to invest in modern pavers. Each contractor used the equipment for perhaps, only 21% of its capability. Costs were thus loaded onto the project and affected the project's viability. The situation saw all the contractors investing in the equipment, when they could have shared. What is important is to specify the use of particular pieces of equipment. The present insistence on ownership locks critical funds into equipment which may remain idle for long. It is the contractor's use of specified equipment that is relevant and this can be a condition to contract. It should be immaterial whether the contractor owns the equipment.

The problem is magnified by restrictions on sale of equipment during the life of the project. Cross-border leasing of equipment and import of second-hand equipment should really take off and these need to be actively facilitated. This will serve several purposes and free up resources. Better yet, as the major investor, the government could also provide the desired equipment to the contractor. There will be enormous savings to the country as a whole since equipment will be utilized to the full.

Apart from efficiency of equipment, there is the issue of efficiency of manpower, both managers and workers. There are several action areas for industry initiatives in this regard. We need to adopt project management systems that increase the efficiency of manpower, materials and machinery, thus reducing cost and enhancing quality.

The NHAI has done phenomenally well when one considers the magnitude of the task and the time frame, but it could achieve even more if it were to attend to a few other areas. In contract documents, there are variations in payment terms on the submission of bill by contractors (from 30–50 days); interest to be paid on delayed payment (7%–12%); amounts of limits on liquidated charge (5%–10% of contract price); and even retention money (variation of 5%–10%) and caps on price adjustment (5%–10%). The contract documents need to be standardized and the time-tested World Bank documents need to be adopted. This will take away the arbitrary differences which occur in contract conditions.

It is equally necessary to standardize the specifications for road projects, as this will enable construction companies to optimize investment in construction equipment and also result in greater transparency and fewer disputes. Finely detailed projects, standardized contract conditions and standardized specifications will result in fewer disputes that are due to ambiguous interpretation. The dispute resolution mechanism is also wanting in the resolution of issues and in moving forward. There is a tendency to disregard awards, which are unfavorable, and even, to challenge the awards routinely. This attitude is not in the spirit of accelerating development in roads infrastructure in the shortest time frame possible.

Insurance covers for construction are typically available for machinery breakdowns, Act of God delays at the construction stage, third-party claims and terrorist-related issues. Insurance covers are not available for delays in the awarding, construction and completion of projects; clients' defaults on payments; financial problems; labor strikes; logistic problems; environmental issues; or abandonment of projects.

Another important issue is the return on investment, which is vital for attracting private investment to BOT ('build-operate-transfer') projects. Currently, BOT is not attractive as traffic projections are inaccurate, collection of user charges is a sensitive issue and returns are elusive. Investment is presently funded from cess charges on petrol and diesel, World Bank/ADB funds and market borrowings. But these need to be serviced, ultimately.

The answer lies in annuity-based BOT projects. To service the annuities and debt, and keep the tolls at low levels, the cess on petrol and diesel will have to continue. It would also be prudent to keep a part of the cess in a sinking fund for future maintenance or upgrading works. Cess, tolls and the value addition from increasing property values of surrounding areas should be able to generate enough resources for servicing investors and financiers, and for future growth.

It will not be enough to create world-class roads. India will need world-class vehicles and logistics firms to operate on these roads. This will happen only if the upgrading of roads is not restricted to the Golden Quadrilateral and the NSEW Corridor. The connectivity between ports, state capitals and major industrial areas is equally vital. The road sector in India has surpassed many targets, particularly in the case of national highways. The same may not be true of state highways, since most states are under fiscal duress. But by and large, the scenario is optimistic. The infrastructure boom assures high-value projects and an opportunity for Indian construction to achieve global benchmarks in technical and managerial capabilities.

On the flipside, Indian companies are limited by under-capitalization, high rates of interest and bank guarantees, inability to hire high-tech equipment and an absence of clients' commitment to time-schedules. But overall, it is 'opportunity unlimited' for all. While there are great challenges ahead, these are not insurmountable for strong companies. There is enough business for one and all.

SOCIAL ISSUES

Scenario

Subhashish Gangopadhyay
Director, India Development Foundation

The social agenda is of particular importance to India. Globalization trends, which are evident in all parts of the world, have enormous implications for the social fabric of a country. Today, production and trade are almost completely knowledge-linked, hence wealth distribution increasingly reflects educational opportunity. Countries need to develop a workforce with the skills and assets crucial to the new knowledge-based global economy. Today, more then ever, inequality means perpetual underdevelopment and poverty. Education, health, and corporate social responsibility are at the fore of balancing India's gap between the have's and the have-not's.

Industry, as a major player in the economic development of the country, needs to play a proactive role in strengthening the social foundations of the nation. The role of industry is not to supplant government initiatives but to supplement them.

EDUCATION

Education is a basic human right and is necessary for sustainable social and economic development. Investment in basic education is indispensable for human development. At the individual level, education opens up possibilities that otherwise would be closed—a better chance to lead healthy and productive lives, to participate fully in civic and political affairs, and to defend and protect rights to survival (not least to address the HIV/AIDS pandemic). Education is crucial to poverty reduction because it is an empowering tool that cannot be restricted to the power-holding classes.

As India's literacy rate is only 65%, better education is a pressing subject. The center and provinces can legislate but the primary responsibility for elementary education rests with the provinces. Education, along with 28 other subjects, has been handed over to local agencies for implementation.

There are four levels of school education—primary, upper primary, secondary and higher secondary. Elementary education comprises eight grades, Grades 1-8, for the age group of 6-14 years; primary education, Grades 1-5 for the 6-11 age group; and upper primary, Grades 6-8 (11-14 age group).

There are 156 million children, 3.3 million teachers and about 1 million schools in the elementary education system. There are 190 million children in the age group of 6-14. $17 billion is spent annually on education. The percentage of GDP spent on education is 3.8%.

More than five decades have passed since the Directive Principle of State Policy, contained in Article 45 of the Constitution of India, stated:

> "The State shall endeavour to provide within a period of ten years from the commencement of this Constitution, free and compulsory education for all children until they complete the age of fourteen years."

However, this goal has proved elusive! As per the Working Group's *Report on Elementary and Adult Education* from the Department of Elementary Education and Literacy, Ministry of Human Resource Development, Government of India, the decade of the 1990s could be called the watershed decade as far as basic education is concerned. Provisional results of the 2001 Census show the highest jump of 13.17% in literacy rate since 1951, with the rate going up from 52.21% in 1991 to 65.38% in 2001.

More significantly, for the first time, the absolute figures of illiterates have gone down by 3.19 crores in spite of an increasing population, while the number of literates has gone up by a phenomenal 20.36 crores.

Presently, nearly three-quarters of the male population and more than half of the female population are literate. All states, without exception, have shown increases in literacy rate during this decade with male literacy exceeding 60% of the male population.

Another significant feature of the nineties is the narrowing gender gap. While male literacy went up by only 11.72% in the nineties, female literacy went up by 14.87% in the same period.

In elementary education too, progress towards universalization has been significant. Concerted efforts towards UEE have resulted in manifold increases in institutions, teachers and students.

Since 1993, the situation, with regard to access to the primary stage, has improved considerably because of interventions of centrally-sponsored schemes like Operation Blackboard, the District Primary Education Programme, the Non-Formal Education and Education Guarantee Scheme, and the efforts of state governments. However, there are still many small and inaccessible regions where there are inadequate schooling facilities.

Total enrollment at the primary stage increased by 5.91 times between 1950 and 1951, and between 1999 and 2000; the increase was 9.16 times for girls. The Gross Enrolment Ratio (GER) at the primary level increased from 42.6% in 1950/51 to 94.90% in 1999/2000. However, large disparities exist between the states in terms of enrollment, and educationally-backward states have lower GER than the total average of India.

The dropout rate has been decreasing year after year in primary classes—from 65% in 1960/61 to 40.25% in 1999/2000. Similarly, in the upper primary classes, the dropout rate has decreased from 78% in 1960/61 to 54.53% in 1999/2000.

In addition, a substantial increase in the number of teachers has been registered since 1950/51. However, the teacher-pupil ratio has worsened since the increase in teacher recruitment has not been able to keep pace with increased enrollment.

A large percentage of the Indian population resides in rural areas and their children attend government schools. The 1968 policy had envisaged that the common school system would be open to all children irrespective of social, economic and other differences, that adequate standards would be maintained, and that parents with average incomes would not feel the need to send their children to expensive schools outside the system.

Similar systems have developed in other democracies such as the neighborhood school system in the USA and the comprehensive school system in the UK. This is not true of the Indian education system.

Social discrimination is still rampant in the Indian school system. Different types of schooling opportunities are available to different sections of the population. The poor and the disadvantaged attend government schools and the well-off students go to private schools. Some children attend formal schools, but for those for whom the formal system is not 'suitable', they attend 'informal' or non-formal educational centers.

Most of these systems have developed in the name of social justice, equal opportunities and deficiency in resources. They are expected to serve the educational interests of the groups they have been established for, but the fact of the matter is that these systems are actually detrimental to the principles of equal opportunity. The child who is poor can never demand a school similar to the one available for the well-to-do child and would inevitably be forced to settle with poor quality education in the government-run primary schools.

Further, the plight of government schools is known to one and all. Thousands of students in primary schools run by local agencies do not have access to safe drinking water, electricity, lavatories, playgrounds, furniture and even, proper premises.

Coupled with this are various systemic issues like poorly functioning schools, high teacher absenteeism, large number of teacher vacancies, poor quality of education and inadequate funds. Other concerns include low enrollment and retention rates, high dropout rates, lack of accessibility and low achievement rates of students.

Unless and until these unmet needs are catered to, the assets on the balance sheet of human resource development will not be able to overpower the liabilities, and the pace of economic growth and development will be slower in spite of investments made in the other sectors.

A blueprint for the future of India's education system must address some of these concerns in a creative and innovative manner so that India is better able to compete globally.

The process for change is an extremely complex one and must address the diversity among the various regions, ethnic groups, sects, castes and classes. The government must commit itself to developing a national plan of action which must be transparent and democratically-negotiated with all significant national stakeholders. The plan must focus on how to achieve national education goals within the broad framework of the 2015 targets and within the government's expenditure framework.

HEALTH

As India is the second most populous country in the world (supporting a population of more than one billion people) and occupies 2.4% of the world's land area, health is of particular concern. The demographic transition has increased the percentage of the population in the 15-60 age group and altered life expectancy. The epidemiological transition has brought an equal burden of non-communicable diseases. All these changes have led to a healthcare scenario challenged by emerging and re-emerging diseases which continue to affect all strata of society.

Communicable diseases stand on the threshold of a new era in which millions of people will be safe from some of them, such as poliomyelitis, leprosy and neonatal tetanus which will join smallpox and guinea-worm as diseases of the past. On the other hand, the crisis of communicable diseases still abounds.

Some infectious diseases thought to be all but conquered have returned with a vengeance or have developed a stubborn resistance to antibiotic drugs—viral hepatitis, syphilis, TB, malaria and pneumonia. To compound this problem, new and previously unknown diseases continue to emerge—HIV/AIDS, the Ebola virus, food and waterborne diseases due to new micro-organisms, and influenza.

The imbalance between health needs and resources is further widened by expanded health conditions. The objective is to achieve an acceptable standard of good health among the general population of the country. It should be a further goal to increase access to the decentralized public health system by establishing new infrastructure in deficient areas and by upgrading infrastructure in the existing institutions.

Both the National Population Policy 2000 and the National Health Policy 2002 aim to achieve population stabilization at a level consistent with the requirements of sustainable economic growth, social development and environmental protection.

Any expectation of a significant improvement in the quality of health services and the consequential improved health status of the citizenry would depend not only upon increased financial and material inputs, but also on a more empathetic and committed attitude on the part of the entire society. Health services would actually need to be delivered by the participating groups in the health sector—public or private, NGOs or other funding agencies.

The attainment of improved health levels would also depend on complementary efforts from areas in the social sector, such as improved drinking water supply, basic sanitation, minimum nutrition. This vision is possible to achieve if pursued as a national movement—requiring constant and effective dialogue among a diversity of stakeholders (collaboration and commitment from the industry) and coordination at all levels of society.

Health is essential not only to the well-being of individuals but to the functioning of economies. Poor health among the work force is a threat to the viability of enterprises and the national stock of human capital

Corporates can and need to be powerful advocates for health. They can take the first step towards advocacy and engaging with the community as part of a broader corporate responsibility agenda.

CORPORATE SOCIAL RESPONSIBILITY

Indian corporations have had a long history of involvement with philanthropic activities and social responsibility. In modern times, it started with the nationalist movement. It is this awareness of the community around them that prompted Indian industrialists to come up with the now-famous Bombay Plan immediately after achieving independence. In the fifties, many business houses established voluntary service organizations to carry out various social activities. India also hosted an international conference on *Social Responsibility of Business*, way back in 1965.

Indeed, in times of natural calamities like famines, droughts, floods and earthquakes, the corporate sector has always stood shoulder-to-shoulder with the government, non-governmental organizations (NGOs) and international relief organizations.

In this regard, big businesses in India have always viewed themselves as more than simply the creators of wealth. According to a CII-UNDP survey carried out in 2002, most corporations feel that social responsibility is not the exclusive domain of the government.

More importantly, the general feeling is that 'passive philanthropy' is no longer sufficient to demonstrate Corporate Social Responsibility (CSR). This obviously raises the question of what good CSR is. Are the corporations doing enough of it? How can it be done more effectively?

The most important question, however, is whether the corporate sector should be involved in CSR at all. Being involved in CSR is a managerial decision. At most, a handful of insider shareholders may participate in such decisions. A large number of small shareholders are certainly not consulted when such actions are taken. Managers can be accused of using company resources to satisfy their own 'feel good' preferences, instead of using these resources to add to the company's, and hence, shareholders' wealth. This can put expenditures on CSR at par with private benefits appropriated by managers. In the interests of good corporate governance, therefore, it is important to convince oneself that CSR will benefit shareholders, before it can be argued that it is good to be a responsible corporate citizen.

First, viewing CSR as an agency cost—managerial private benefit at the shareholders' expense—begs the question of why companies publicize such activities.

If CSR is for the manager's own satisfaction, and he uses up the resources of the company, the last thing a manager would want to do is publicize it. Since shareholders are also getting this information, it is unlikely that they will continue with a manager who squanders company resources. Thus, if managers continue with CSR, and make a fuss about it, it must be because they feel that shareholders want them to do so. Shareholders may like managers to undertake CSR for either one of two reasons—because they feel good that they own companies which are socially-conscious or they feel CSR actually helps the company's bottomline.

There is growing empirical literature which suggests that companies involved in CSR are more profitable than others and their shares are valued higher. This was first demonstrated for firms that actively helped in the betterment of the environment. These are firms that routinely over-comply on regulatory standards, champion the development of environmentally-friendly technologies, and help in raising awareness among the community. Subsequently, such a relationship has also been found in other areas of social activity undertaken by corporations. The inescapable conclusion is that shareholders are aware that CSR is good business.

It could still be that efficient managers are also 'good' persons who are willing to use the resources they manage for a greater cause. Good managers take their ability and independence to undertake CSR as the incentive to be more efficient and hence generate more resources, some of which go back to the shareholders. In other words, efficient managers are always socially-conscious. A stronger case for CSR can be made if it can be demonstrated that involvement in CSR is actually what makes the company more profitable. That is, efficiency demands that managers undertake CSR. CSR then becomes a part of the business strategy. Economics and management literature suggest that CSR often leads to, and seldom is a result of, a company's profitability. Expenditure on CSR is, indeed, good business.

But even if companies can make more profit because of CSR, is it the best way to make these extra profits? It is here that the theoretical literature on firm behavior becomes important. It is not surprising that, in a world where consumers are becoming increasingly aware, they can compel the government to put in place good corporate behavior and alienate companies that do not voluntarily disclose their social activities. CSR is not simply an alternative strategy; it is a necessary practice. Indeed, with the IT revolution, it is impossible to hide socially bad, or even indifferent, activity.

Comment

Carol Bellamy
former Executive Director, United Nations Children's Fund (UNICEF)

India is clearly an important world power. With over 1 billion people, accounting for 16% of global population, and occupying 2.4% of world land area, its sheer size alone is significant.

What, though, is 'new' about India as a 'world power'? In an era where 'brand' reigns, what is India's 'brand'? What do people think of when they see that something is 'made in India'?

Around the world, when people think about India, they may think of its growing IT and bio-tech industries; they think of outsourcing; they think of population size; they think of a stunning breadth of culture, history, music and dance; and it is likely that they also think of poverty. Recently, they have started thinking of India as likely to be the next biggest center of the AIDS explosion in the world.

While many have heard about India's economic growth, few are aware of India's changing demographics. Between 1951 and 2000, life expectancy increased from 36.7 to 64.6 years, while infant mortality rate fell from 146 to 70 deaths per 1,000 in the same period. In other words, on one hand, India is seeing an increasingly older population, and on the other, more than half its population are still only under 25 years old. India has a high maternal mortality ratio, averaging 540 pregnancy-related deaths per 100,000 live births. This statistic has not improved over the past decade.

India's economic growth and business trends are discussed in the other essays in this important volume. What I will discuss here is the potential social dimensions of India's growth, building on the discussions around Corporate Social Responsibility (CSR), education and health 'blueprints' developed in this book.

The recommendations on social issues that are outlined in the Scenario underline three key directions, all of which are built on an underlying agreed principle that growth needs to be inclusive, with equal opportunities for all, to improve the total quality of life for all Indians. The three key recommendations were to:

1) invest in the development of human capital
2) improve the social infrastructure—health, education, clean water
3) tackle the HIV/AIDS situation

If all these recommendations are realized, India will be a truly significant world power.

Recognizing that sustainable growth will depend on a stable social infrastructure, key questions to consider are: what are the implications of the recent economic growth for the social sector—the foundation for any sustained growth and development? How can this economic growth be re-invested to strengthen India's infrastructure and human capital in order to allow for continued growth? In UNICEF's language, how will economic growth contribute to creating a nation 'Fit for Children'? And in addition, what can the business sector contribute?

Investing in the development of 'human capital' is a key recommendation. It motivates the other recommendations to 'improve the social infrastructure', namely, infrastructure to deliver clean water, provide healthcare facilities, make education accessible and to 'tackle HIV/AIDS'—all of which are critical investments towards developing human capital.

Faced with such vast needs, how do businesses start to assess where they may invest?

The education and health 'blueprints' profile India's overall education and its health status. Both reflect notable improvements over the past 50 years, but also point to significant and remaining gaps in the access to, as well as, poor quality of, services. While they present a broader national picture, they are indicative of areas where additional investment is needed.

EDUCATION

The education profile in India is a mix of wonderful gains and significant remaining challenges.

As outlined in the education blueprint, the Gross Enrolment Ratio (GER) at the primary school level increased over 50% in the past 50 years, reaching well over 90% in 2000. Although the trend is positive, large disparities exist between and within states. Reaching the yet unreached remains a challenge, along with the huge issue of quality—an underlying factor that influences school attendance. The *Human Development Report (2003)* reports that only 68% of primary school attendees complete fifth grade.

Literacy rates have also increased over time and the gap between male and female literacy is narrowing, although female literacy rates still lag behind. In addition, the overall teacher-student ratio has become worse as teacher recruitment has not kept up with increases in enrollment. This suggests that even though more children may be attending school, the quality of education is poor, given the limited availability of teachers. Poor building conditions and inadequate access to safe drinking water and sanitation facilities are also persistent concerns.

Those who can afford to often opt out of public education for private alternatives. But, for those who cannot afford to pursue private education, education is particularly vital to help remove income disparities. The poor have little or no economic capital and rely on human capital to pull themselves out of poverty. Education is essential.

Education is a key underlying factor for any sustainable growth and development. It is important not only for job opportunities or to build a literate consumer population, it is a critical factor which has repeatedly been shown to contribute to better health, productivity and well-being, and the ability to negotiate in an increasingly competitive world.

Girls' education is known to be a particularly vital investment. Regions that have invested over the long-term in girls' education, such as Southeast Asia, have shown higher levels of economic development. Evidence shows that as primary school enrollment for girls increases, gross domestic product per capita follows.

The *2004 State of the World's Children Report* discusses the 'multiplier effect' of education in contributing to better health and protection from abuse and exploitation. The report noted that with each year that the mother is educated, the mortality rate of her children under five is only between 5 and 10%.

The recommendations underline the importance of inclusiveness and equal opportunities for all. Businesses can play the role of an advocate for those who have less of a voice, calling for basic education and health services to reach the unreached, and bringing attention to the importance of a strong education system for economic growth.

India's reputation and 'brand'—behind the headlines on new growth and outsourcing—still provoke images of poverty, inadequate health and education services. The *Global Competitiveness Report (2003-2004)* identified 'inadequate infrastructure' as the most problematic factor affecting business in India, followed by 'inefficient bureaucracy'. The quality of public institutions, such as educational institutions, is not just a social welfare issue; it is clearly integral to business competitiveness and economic growth.

HEALTH

The health blueprint outlined a scenario of 'epidemiological transition' in which India is still challenged by traditional communicable diseases while facing the emergence of relatively new diseases such as HIV/AIDS, drug-resistant strains of old diseases such as TB and malaria, and an increase of non-communicable diseases.

The productivity of the workplace is clearly affected by the issue of health—not only the immediate health of individual workers, but also the health of their families and community. Workers' absenteeism is not only due to their own illness, it may also be due to the need to care for sick family members.

The blueprint points to the example of tuberculosis (TB), which particularly affects 15-45 year-olds, the most economically productive age group. TB costs India approximately US$3 billion every year in terms of lost productivity as well as costs of treatment. On average, 15 years of income is lost if an individual dies from TB. This is the scenario for an illness that can be cured with six months of relatively inexpensive treatment. Imagine AIDS. No cure, just lifelong drugs.

The implications of an unchecked HIV/AIDS epidemic for India's sustained growth are yet to be seen, but the recommendation 'to tackle the HIV/AIDS situation' is undoubtedly the most urgent of the recommendations that needs to be addressed. There is still time to slow the epidemic whose potential impact could set India back by many development years.

What are the particular areas that could benefit from support by the business sector? HIV/AIDS is certainly an area that needs considerable scaling up of attention—both prevention and care—in order to avert a major epidemic and significant repercussions on gains made. One starting point is certainly among company employees. Investment in HIV/AIDS prevention and care in local communities is another tangible, much-needed intervention that has significant implications for the future.

A laudable example of corporate social responsibility—and good business sense—is Tata Tea Limited (TTL)'s investment in HIV/AIDS prevention and care. TTL started a workplace HIV/AIDS program that initially covered 29 tea estates in India and involved a total of 27,000 employees (46% of all TTL employees). TTL saw an increase in HIV-related deaths among its employees and assessed that the conditions were present for a further increase. In response, they partnered with a local health project and the National AIDS Control Organization (NACO) to support an HIV program primarily focused on education, prevention, raising awareness, as well as, voluntary counselling and testing (VCT), and a wellness program.

TTL estimated that each HIV+ infection would cost the company $8,000, which is eight times the average annual wage. The costs were estimated at 45% due to lost productivity, 30% medical treatment, 15% death benefits and 10% lost training investment. Without any prevention or care intervention, TTL anticipated that the HIV prevalence among its workers could increase 3% in five years.

Policy is another key part of the TTL HIV/AIDS initiative. The workplace HIV/AIDS policy focused particularly on issues surrounding non-discrimination, confidentiality and disclosure, benefits and termination.

Tangible interventions in the program included having a vice president as a significant advocate in increasing awareness, training of peer educators, community outreach programs, targeted outreach activities to high-risk populations, and condom dispensers in the workplace.

The key success factors of the TTL experience included an in-depth local needs assessment, leveraging existing and available health services and infrastructure, flexible funding arrangements, regular involvement of the management and a well-balanced team comprising key stakeholders.

In addressing the recommendation to 'tackle the HIV/AIDS situation', the TTL lesson is one that can inspire others.

CORPORATE SOCIAL RESPONSIBILITY

The principle of 'corporate social responsibility' and its importance was recognized by all in the discussions and reiterated in the principles outlined in the Corporate Social Responsibility 'blueprint'. That the business sector should invest in the social sector is no longer seen as a luxury, but as a need for a company's productivity.

'Social responsibility' can include being environmentally-sensitive, following good manufacturing practices, and respecting labor laws that protect the rights, health and well-being of employees. It can also mean taking leadership on social issues that are not immediately related to the company's productivity. While 'social responsibility' needs to be owned across both public and private sectors, business clearly has a key role to play. Companies can, for instance, partner the government and become important advocates in influencing public policy on social concerns.

Good relations with and investment in communities where businesses operate also affect a company's image and people's willingness—and ability—to buy its products or services. Studies show that the overall morale of employees is higher when they feel that they work for a fundamentally good, caring company that is investing in the well-being of people.

The notion of 'corporate social responsibility' is not new to India. What is new is an understanding that it is integral—not additional—to good business.

MOVING FORWARD

The recent economic growth has given a boost of confidence that growth is happening and change is possible. India is very much engaged in a quickly-changing world, ahead of the curve in some ways, but still behind in others. The 'others' are not only the traditional development needs of investing in education, health, water and sanitation, but newer concerns such as HIV/AIDS.

When I reflect on the overall upbeat mood and the recommendations (which were optimistic, but also sobering in acknowledging the remaining challenges ahead), I think of the images of the 'Incredible India' campaign that greet travelers at the airports.

Wouldn't it be a truly 'incredible India' if current growth continued, health services reached the poorest, every child goes to school and every school is adequately staffed?

Wouldn't it be an incredible India if the country showed the world that it has learned the lessons of other countries and reined in the emerging AIDS epidemic through a remarkable partnership of private and public entities, of businesses and communities?

Wouldn't it be an incredible India if all this were finally achieved, or at least exponential progress made?

It would be an India 'Fit for Children'—for ALL India's children.

Comment

Jamshyd Godrej
Chairman and Managing Director, Godrej & Boyce Manufacturing, India

When compared to its neighbors in the East, India's economic growth rate in the last 55 years has been less than spectacular. In the initial years, the emphasis was on building 'temples of modern India' as Jawaharlal Nehru termed them. These were huge public investments in basic manufacturing such as in steel, heavy engineering and refineries. Large numbers of investment projects were given to the public sector. The nationalization of banks and the insurance sector prevented public finance from reaching the private sector.

This emphasis on industrial development sucked resources away from the development of social and physical infrastructure. Inadequate investment in infrastructure such as roads, ports and airports led to poor interconnectivity, especially in rural areas.

The social sector as well as primary education and healthcare received scant attention. Primary education did not receive the same attention that higher education did. But today, there are world-class colleges, institutes of technology and institutes of management.

Poor public education on family planning and illiteracy, especially amongst women, led to high birth rates, which were most pronounced in north India—Uttar Pradesh, Bihar, Rajasthan and Madhya Pradesh.

The farm-based economy gradually led to an industrial-based and service sector-oriented economy. Today, the GDP consists of approximately 50% in services and 25% each in industry and agriculture. Further, about 70% of India's population is still involved in agriculture. The agricultural sector is dependent on highly subsidized power, water and fertilizers, among other things. This has tied down investments in social infrastructure in rural areas.

Successive governments have paid lip service to the development of social and physical infrastructure. In the last few years, there has been a greater appreciation that unless the basic ingredients of development, i.e. social and physical infrastructure, are developed rapidly, future growth prospects for the Indian economy could be bleak. Until now, the governments at the central, state, regional and local levels have been the main providers of social infrastructure. But as Rajiv Gandhi once famously said, "80% of the funds for social development did not reach the beneficiaries."

A NEW PARADIGM

Under these circumstances, what is required is a new paradigm for developing social infrastructure. The experience of empowering panchayats has not been successful so far.

The corporate sector has gradually gotten involved in providing social infrastructure. Many large companies that are established in rural and semi-rural areas such as Tata Steel have invested large amounts in schools, colleges, hospitals, healthcare and family planning centers, etc.

The time has come to empower the corporate sector through encouragement and direct funding of social infrastructure in specific areas of operation. The corporate sector reaches a large percentage of population directly and indirectly, and could be mobilized for this purpose.

Today, India is still threatened by diseases such as tuberculosis, leprosy, HIV/AIDS and malaria. The corporate sector's involvement in tackling these has been significant.

I am proposing a new partnership between governments at all levels and the corporate sector to make significant headway in the setting up of primary schools, secondary schools, basic healthcare facilities, and basic rural hospitals, etc. At the same time, the government must intensify the road building projects that are already underway so that connectivity in rural areas through various social infrastructure projects could improved.

ROLE OF TECHNOLOGY

There is a role for technology in providing education and healthcare in rural areas. The Indian Space Research Organisation (ISRO) has recently launched an education satellite, 'EDUSAT', to provide satellite-based connectivity to rural areas throughout India. Experienced and expert teachers could provide lessons on far-ranging topics via the satellite. In addition to basic literacy lessons, they could cover topics such as water conservation and agricultural products, among others. Ground-breaking demonstration projects in the healthcare sector have also shown that trained village girls could take care of 80% of the basic healthcare needs of the village. Satellite technology-based connectivity enables training in what to do in complicated cases and provides access to information on the availability of facilities for patients, among other things.

Unless we experiment with new models and use modern communication technology, the task of providing basic social infrastructure is a daunting one. The president of India, Dr. APJ Abdul Kalam has presented a framework for rural connectivity and development. Technology would provide the basic information connectivity; rural roads would provide the basic movement of goods and people; development of social infrastructure would provide the fuel for development; entrepreneurial ideas would provide employment; and, timely and expert advice on agriculture would allow more efficient use of resources. These areas of excellence could in time transform the rural areas.

There are a large number of private sector institutions in education and healthcare. Currently, these are mostly in the urban and semi-urban areas. The private sector needs to be encouraged to take over the development of the entire social infrastructure in urban and semi-urban areas so that state resources are freed for rural and semi-rural areas. The corporate sector that operates in rural and semi-rural areas could also be encouraged to take over the running of social infrastructure in these areas. In this way, there could be a transformation in the provision of primary education and basic healthcare. There is also a very significant role for non-government organizations (NGOs) in the implementation and running of these initiatives in education and healthcare.

JOB CREATION

Reforms and new initiatives in the Indian economy have so far been focused on the development of industry and service sectors. Due to global competition, the emphasis has been on productivity and efficiency. The corporate sector has hence been unable to create new jobs in adequate numbers. China developed a strategy of rapidly developing its coastal areas. In an export-based economy, this created millions of jobs and attracted large numbers of people from the hinterland. In addition, China emphasized the development of basic infrastructure such as road, ports and airports, etc. This enabled the Chinese economy to grow at an exceptionally fast rate.

India too needs to emulate China in developing basic infrastructure and creating employment opportunities for export-based industries which are labor-intensive. Export-based industries need good connectivity to sea-ports and airports. Also, good roads and rail systems should be provided. These export industries could be based in rural and semi-rural areas within 100 kilometers of the ports. The social infrastructure developed in these rural and semi-rural areas which are around the export zones would provide human capital for the industries. This would result in a virtuous cycle of employment, skills development and human development.

The corporate sector has demonstrated that there are highly competitive knowledge-based, technology-based and employment-based companies in various industry sectors. Those that have emerged winners are highly competitive in cost in a global context. These areas of excellence could spread and trigger similar levels of global competitiveness amongst all sectors of the economy.

This new model of social infrastructure development, rapid industrial expansion, and efficient and sustainable use of resources will provide employment to millions upon millions of people.

Part 3

Conclusions

ENVISIONING THE FUTURE

by Tarun Das

The goal of this book is to present scenarios for India's future. From our assessments, we feel that India will have a great future.

First, India's economic conditions are sustainable and stable enough to allow for the kind of sustainable growth that the government in Delhi has set itself. India's competitive factors—its young population, entrepreneurial spirit and democratic institutions—remain strong for the future.

Secondly, India continues to be one of the most politically stable countries in Asia. For this reason, the country will be able to attract a big portion of global foreign direct investment.

Thirdly, India's economic success has earned respect from the developing world. This enhances India's position in the international arena. India should be considered a pivotal state in a world much challenged by the need for bridges across seemingly intractable divides.

As we look ahead, the prospects are good. Like other journeys, the one India will take to reach its future destination will inevitably be filled with some degree of uncertainty and obstacles. Nevertheless, as most contributors to this book agreed, India is ready—physically and mentally—to embark on this journey.

The origin of the Indian manufacturing industry goes back to the 19th century, and is linked to the railway system. In the period after India's Independence in 1947, the industry witnessed steady growth. The industrial base was diversified and the emergence of the public sector reflected the beginnings of the capital goods and heavy industry base in the country.

Generally speaking, the 1947-1991 period was a time when industrial development and growth was regulated, planned, controlled and directed. This was due to the scarcity of resources and the perceived need to use limited resources according to set priorities.

The outcome of this process was a mix of public and private sector industry, including a vast array of small and medium industries. To foster and nurture the small industry network, and to promote entrepreneurship, nearly 900 product lines were reserved for the small industries.

Another dimension of planned industrial development was seen in the protection from foreign competition given by the state to local firms. Tariffs were high. There were import controls on goods. Capacity licensing was observed in an attempt to match supply/demand situations. Planned development led to growth but it also had an unfortunate by-product. The lack of competition bred complacency in industry. Product and service quality were less than desirable. Prices for the buyer were high. The customer was neglected. This was the natural result of a lack of competitive pressures.

In the late 1970s and early 1980s, an effort was made to relax import controls and licensing. But this was extremely limited in nature. In 1985, the government attempted to move this process forward but again, the exercise was far from complete. However, 1985 did witness a new initiative to modernize industry, use technology, develop IT and create a vision of a different type of Indian industry—more outward–looking and more innovative.

Anticipating the advent of competition, Indian industry began to focus on quality and competitiveness in 1988. Across Indian industry, a steady movement began, focusing on the need to improve performance, productivity and quality.

And, when in 1991, the real beginning of deregulation, de-licensing and de-control dawned, industry was somewhat partly prepared for the emergence of a competitive market.

Between 1991 and 1996 (the first five years of this new paradigm of developments when controls were being steadily dismantled), industry experienced high growth and profitability. The economy reached 7% GDP growth over a three-year period and industry began to enjoy the new experience—investing heavily, building new capacities and learning to operate differently.

In 1997, the Asian Economic Crisis took place, bringing with it new pain and pressure. Growth declined and in fact, stagnated. The pressure of imports added to the problems of a still largely un-competitive industry. The cry for slowing down liberalization as well as the urging for safeguards and protection grew. Industries were closing down. Employees were losing their jobs. It was a difficult time for the manufacturing industry in India.

However, there were two silver linings. First, there was a positive boom in the Indian IT industry. India's software companies began making their presence felt in the world, especially in the U.S. economy. India's engineering and technical skills blew across the American continents. The U.S. industry, which has a reputation for technology and innovation, started using Indian software skills to enhance their own competitiveness. A new era of achievement in Indian industry had begun, an era based on intellectual knowledge and technical skills of India's human resources.

The second silver lining was the effective restructuring process in the manufacturing industry. The process began in the 1990s, and was deepened, and sharpened post-1997. Companies across the country and across sectors reviewed their businesses and operations, restructured their organizations and 'right-sized' their workforce. By 2002, a new industrial force was emerging.

A new phase of development in the Indian industry began in 2003. It had several new dimensions.

The manufacturing industry showed new competitiveness in spite of steadily falling tariffs and abolition of import controls. The whining and crying for protection was at a minimum and the ability to perform efficiently and globally became a new phenomenon. With competitiveness came confidence. And with the liberalization of foreign exchange controls, industry went beyond exports to invest internationally in key markets.

In the pre-1991 period, a few corporates had invested abroad but these were extremely limited and restricted to a few sectors such as textiles. In the post-2000 period, investments extended to pharmaceuticals, automotive components, minerals, electronics, software and others. These are still early days but the growing trend of investments in Greenfield sites or acquisitions gives clear indication of a rising number of Indian corporates venturing out of Fortress India. The manufacturing industry in India, for the first time, was looking globally competitive.

On the other hand, the services sector, especially software, experienced its first pangs of real pain. Linked closely to U.S. industry, the software companies were hit hard by the slowdown in the U.S. economy, the cutbacks in spending on IT, the downturn in Silicon Valley and the problems of U.S. corporates.

As if this was not enough, a new problem emerged—the reaction to outsourcing which was linked to the loss of jobs in the U.S.

The Indian software industry responded with speed and efficiency. Restructuring, cost control and business review happened overnight and, after a brief dip in results, the IT leaders came back on a strong growth path in terms of turnover and profitability. The industry also rapidly diversified its markets, penetrating Europe, Japan, China and Southeast Asia, among other regions.

A major outcome of the changes in the business environment in the 1990s and the early years of the 21st century has been the sense of comfort felt with technology. Shedding old habits and old technologies, Indian corporates embraced the new ways of doing business using up-to-date technology, especially in IT.

Another outcome was with regard to business strategy itself. Earlier, the trend was to go in for joint ventures to access technology. More recently, after many joint ventures could not be sustained, Indian corporates understood the need to go it alone. This also applied to foreign companies coming into India. In an increasingly competitive environment in India, both MNCs and Indian companies have realized that the best strategy was to manage on their own.

There is, therefore, a new climate in Indian industry. Growth rates for manufacturing and services are near 10% per annum and likely to be sustained because of domestic growth at 7% GDP and access to global markets. Clearly, there will be ups and downs in the future, but there is an understanding that enhancing competitiveness is a continuing process. There is also a new realization that Indian companies have the ability to make the grade and be competitive.

A more encouraging aspect is the transformation in the SME sector. Faced with the challenges of competition, small and midsized companies are cooperating with their counterparts in clusters to build their own competitiveness. This approach is already showing very positive results.

Finally, the people factor—workers, executives, engineers, scientists, entrepreneurs and others. Under the pressures of competition and in an industry-friendly environment, India's human resource is globally competitive and capable.

India has realized this. The world has realized this. The 1.2 billion population can be an asset, not a liability, given education and training. The exciting part is that over 50% of India's population is under 25 years of age and full of energy, enthusiasm and excitement. They will propel India into a new age of development and growth.

INDEX